Healing Ourselves, Healing Our Children

Stories about parenting by parents affected by the child welfare system

By Rise
Edited by Nora McCarthy

Rise

Editor
Nora McCarthy

Layout & Design
Jeff Faerber

Cover Art
Elizabeth Deegan

ISBN 978-1-933939-99-5

Printed in the United States of America

Rise®
New York, New York
www.risemagazine.org

About Rise

Rise trains parents to write about their experiences with the child welfare system in order to support parents and parent advocacy and to guide child welfare practitioners and policymakers in becoming more responsive to the families and communities they serve.

Our print magazine, Rise, reaches 18,000 parents nationwide. We work with family support and child welfare agencies to use Rise stories in support groups and parenting education classes. We partner with parent advocacy organizations to use Rise stories in child welfare reform. Learn more about Rise at our website, www.risemagazine.org.

CONTENTS

Introduction

How to use this book in parenting classes and support groups.

Our parenting education and support resources are designed to help you easily integrate parents' stories into your work. You can integrate stories into parenting classes or parent support groups, or easily design a new group using Rise stories.

Choosing Stories: Stories in this book focus on establishing close, positive relationships with young children and establishing safe, structured home lives. Parents who grew up in unstable homes or whose children have been in foster care or are at risk of entering the child welfare system need support in re-learning to parent their children and developing confidence about their ability to safely care for their children.

Use Rise Stories to Build Rapport

Most group work begins with activities to build a sense of safety and rapport with group participants. Reading a Rise story on a general topic you will cover in the group can help establish that parents' perspectives and knowledge will be honored in your group and can help everyone in the group feel less alone. It can help your parenting class or support group start out from a place of trust and confidence.

After a simple introductory exercise, like a game to remember people's names, or an overview of what you hope to accomplish in the group or class, pass out copies of a story that relates to your group. Ask volunteers to each read a short section of the story. You can open up a discussion using the discussion guide, or by asking simple questions that will help the group find common ground: What can you relate to about this story? What did the writer do that you might like to try?

Use Rise Stories to Bring a Child Welfare Focus to Parent Education

If you are using a general parenting curriculum, use Rise stories to tailor the class to the needs and concerns of parents who are with children in foster care or at risk of entering the child welfare system. Parents who feel unsure whether they can try the new parenting techniques or styles will be shored up by reading about the experiences of other parents who learned new parenting skills in order to change negative family patterns. To add Rise stories to a parenting education curriculum, match our topics to the weekly parenting concepts you will cover in your group. Rise stories can bring a child welfare focus to a general parenting class.

Use Rise Stories to Enhance Cultural Competency

Many child welfare-affected parents are skeptical of techniques taught in parenting classes, which they see as reflecting a white or middle-class style. Most of our stories are written by low-income black and Latino parents. Rise stories demonstrate how these parents have found comfortable solutions to parenting dilemmas. Integrate our stories into your parenting curriculum or hand out stories for parents to read at home to bring realistic and culturally appropriate case studies to your classes.

Use Rise Stories to Create a Parenting Support Group

To bring some structure to support groups in which parents take the lead in supporting, guiding and encouraging each other, consider beginning some or all discussions by reading a Rise story. Reading a story can set an open, thoughtful tone and help parents feel more comfortable opening up. Filling out the worksheet can help participants think through steps they may want to take based on ideas raised in the support group discussion. If you are setting up a new support group, you can ask parent participants to identify their goals or the topics they would like to discuss and match our stories to their needs. You can also use the stories in the order suggested in this workbook.

Overview: How to Use the Discussion Guides

Prepare by photocopying the story and journal reflection worksheet for each participant. Develop the discussion by following these steps:

1) Read aloud the paragraph-long introduction to explain the day's topic to your group.

2) Hand out copies of the story.

3) Ask group members to take turns reading short sections of the story out loud.

4) Use our suggested discussion questions tied to specific story moments to help group members open up about their own experiences.

5) Hand out journal reflection worksheets that accompany each story. These help parent participants reflect on their own experiences and write down the steps they would like to take in applying what they've learned.

6) Ask participants to complete the reflection questions and action steps in the group or at home. Participants can share their responses with the group, with a partner in the group, with their lawyer or therapist, or another resource they identify.

(Reading and discussion time: 45 minutes-1 hour. Worksheet completion and discussion time 15-45 minutes.)

Like Daughter, Like Mother

Learning confidence from my daughter.

By Margarita Pavon

Translated from Spanish

When I was six years old, the same age that my daughter is now, my mother left me with my grandmother. Nearly every evening I would peek out in the street to see if my mother had arrived. But six years passed and she didn't come back. I missed her so much.

Even though my grandmother was attentive to my needs, it wasn't easy. When I wanted to share something with my mother or ask her a question, she wasn't there. I needed a lot from my mother as a child and I feel as if I still need her today.

Afraid to Speak

Finally, when I turned 12, I went to live with my mother again, but our relationship never grew strong. My mother is a woman with an explosive character. It was very difficult for me to adjust to her personality. I never had the confidence to tell my mother what was going on with me. I don't know if it's my nature to be timid, but I don't remember my mother ever asking me, "How was your day?"

My daughter is just the opposite. America (that's her name) is a very pretty little girl with dark, clear skin, long eyelashes, thick eyebrows, and a small mouth. She loves to color, draw and read, but what she likes best is to talk. Even as a baby, she was a screamer. When she wanted her milk, she wanted it instantly and hot. We say that she seems like a parrot. She says, "I'm not a parrot! I just like to talk."

Encouraging My Children

I admire America's confidence. One day I was chatting with my sister-in-law in the kitchen and America came out of her room and told us to be quiet. "The only person that can talk a lot is me. I am the queen!" she told us.

I try to give America and my son, Alan, the confidence that I never had with my mother. I do my best to be loving toward them and to show them that they are important to me by chatting with them about school and their days.

Obviously there are times when I get angry and speak harshly. But when they are fighting, I try to stay calm, saying, "That's not OK. You have to help and take care of each other."

I think that without my realizing it, my grandmother taught me to be the mother I am today. My grandmother was loving, although on occasion a little strict. She always taught us to be well organized, and she tried to teach us patience. She didn't yell at us if we didn't do things right the first time, which my mother often did.

Changing Myself

Sometimes I wish I was more like America. If someone bothers her—Oh! She lets them know. If something makes her uncomfortable, she easily defends herself. She's not afraid to say how she feels.

Me, I don't do that. First I get nervous, and then I cry. I would like to express my feelings without fear of being criticized. I feel afraid of hurting other people if I speak my mind, because I know how that feels. When my mother yelled at me, she said so many terrible things. She didn't care if she hurt my feelings. Those things she said left a mark on me, even though I try not to remember them.

I have tried to become more confident. Now I can ask questions if I need to, without feeling afraid. Whenever we've had people over to the house, I used to stay apart from everyone else. I'm more sociable now.

Tender Moments

My mother and I still don't communicate well. I want to let her know how much I missed her when I was a child and that I wished she could've given me love, confidence and tenderness.

I don't have too many good memories of my childhood. Once my mother brought my sister and me to a circus. I took a picture in which I had on a white blouse and a checkered skirt. I remember this as a moment when I felt happy and content with my mother.

I want to give many moments like that to my children. I still have a lot to learn about being an excellent mother, but I hope that America and Alan will always confide in me.

LEADER'S GUIDE:

Like Daughter, Like Mother by Margarita Pavon
Learning confidence from my daughter.

www.risemagazine.org

DISCUSSION FOCUS:
Desire to connect.

ACTIVITY GOAL:
Participants will define the kind of home environment they want to create for their children.

STORY SUMMARY

As a child, Margarita lives apart from her mother for many years, and is afraid to open up to her when they live together again, even though she craves a stronger, more positive connection. Margarita develops into a shy, worried young woman.

As a parent, she hopes to make it possible for her children to feel connected and close to her. She admires her daughter's confidence and begins to take risks opening up herself.

DISCUSSION GUIDE

GROUP INTRODUCTION: 10 minutes

Today we're going to talk about the home environments we want to create for our children. So many of us felt as children that we wanted our parents to listen to us and that, at times, we felt unsafe or shut down. As parents, we struggle to balance our children's demands with our own needs. Taking even a little time to listen to and notice your children can help you and your children feel close, connected and confident.

- How do you feel about this topic?
- Do you have experiences related to this topic that you'd like to share before we get started?

READ AND DISCUSS STORY: 15 + 30 minutes

Read the story out loud as a group. Help participants recognize the writer's emotions and coping mechanisms and their own. Go back over important moments in the story and ask the participants about how they've handled similar experiences:

STORY MOMENT	DISCUSSION QUESTION
Margarita does not feel safe expressing herself to her mother.	How safe and open was the home environment that you grew up in?
Margarita hopes that her children will grow up feeling more confident and connected to her.	How would like your children to grow up feeling about themselves?
Margarita has tried to create an open environment by talking to her children about their feelings and trying not to get too mad.	How have you tried to create a safe and comfortable environment for your children?
One barrier to creating an open environment is that Margarita herself feels sad, jealous and closed at times.	What barriers—including your own sad or closed feelings—do you face in creating a comfortable home environment?
Margarita is learning from her daughter that it is OK to express her own needs and feelings.	What have you learned from your children?

JOURNAL TIME: 15-30 minutes

By writing in their journals, participants can more deeply reflect on their experiences and the steps they can take to strengthen themselves and their families. Hand out the "Journal Reflections" worksheet and give participants 15-30 minutes to write. They can share their responses with the group or in pairs, or after the workshop with a counselor, therapist, or peer.

NAME: **DATE:**

JOURNAL REFLECTIONS: Like Mother, Like Daughter by Margarita Pavon

Margarita was deeply affected by being separated from her mother and then, when they reconnected, by her mother's harsh parenting style. At the same time, Margarita learned a positive parenting style from her grandmother and tries to be similarly gentle and understanding with her children.

Take some time to reflect on the elements of your childhood that you do and don't want to pass on to your children. Use the questions below to guide your reflections.

1. What connections or activities helped you feel confident and safe as a child?

2. What made you feel unsafe?

3. How do you think you create a safe and comfortable home environment for yourself and your children?

4. What challenges do you face in helping your children feel safe and connected?

____

____

____

____

ACTION STEPS

Simple steps, like creating a time to talk with your child each day, can help you build a close connection. Write down 2-3 steps you could take to help your child feel valued.

1. ____

____

____

2. ____

____

____

3. ____

____

____

A SUPPORTIVE CONNECTION

I plan to get support and encouragement by talking about my reflections and action steps with:

____

Closer Than Ever

I'm learning how to handle my children.

By Sandra Evans

When I was 12, drugs became my way to numb out all the ugly feelings I had inside from being molested and being ignored by my mother, who always put men ahead of her children. Eventually I tried meth and became addicted. Those painful childhood memories, the ones that no one talks about, disappeared with meth.

My addiction escalated when I was about 25 and caring for my four children under age 5. My husband, Francisco, and I lived in a neighborhood in Fresno, Calif., where at every fourth house they either used meth or sold it. Soon getting high became my escape from the smallest things—my baby crying, or a fight with Francisco.

I'm not sure what triggered me to start using so much. Thinking back, I see it may have been a number of things. Francisco was going to school, which left me home alone all day. I found caring for all of our children overwhelming and was jealous that Francisco was bettering his life. My role as a mother seemed insignificant.

Filled With Fear

I also feared that I did not know how to be a mom. I did some things well. I always made sure my children were fed and bathed. We would read together and go to the park by our house. But I was really stressed out because I was afraid of making all the mistakes that my mother had made with me.

My addiction made my parenting worse. I was always frustrated with my children and Francisco. I would yell at my oldest, who was only 5, "Make Emiliano a bottle" or, "Take care of your brothers." Other times I did what I had to do but with no emotion. I had become totally numb.

When I got pregnant again, I knew I needed to quit and I wanted to. I would tell myself, "This hit will be the last," but kept using.

No More Hiding

When my baby was born, child protective services intervened. My husband and I met with the CPS workers and agreed that he would stay home and raise our children while I went to drug treatment with the baby for six months.

The day I was admitted, I felt angry at myself, scared and guilty. I thought, "How did I let it get this far?"

I also felt hopeful. Maybe, just maybe, if I gave this place a try, they could help me deal with all the raw emotions I carried inside. Then I could go home to my children a better mom.

Rebuilding My Family

Through treatment, I got to connect with my family in a much different way than I had before. Francisco and our children came to visit on Saturdays. I looked forward to our visits. I wanted to hear about everything they had been doing.

I would play with our kids, read to them, color and really enjoy our time. These were things I hadn't done with my children too often.

Being in the program with my daughter was a wonderful experience, too. I was able to enjoy taking care of her. We had a special class called Therapeutic Childcare that gave us time and support to bond with our babies.

The teacher, Ms. V., gave me confidence that, despite my childhood, I could raise my children without neglecting them. I tried what she suggested and found that her guidance helped me build a stronger connection with all of my children.

Attention and Consistency

Ms. V. taught us little things that can set the foundation to connect with your children. For instance, I used to make a bottle, put my baby in the bed, prop up the bottle with a blanket, and that was that. She told me that propping the bottle can make a baby choke, get ear infections and have trouble learning to stop eating when she is full. Most important, feeding the baby in your arms is a way you show the baby you love and care about her.

I learned that children thrive when they have a daily schedule and when you're consistent with them. Ms. V. told me that it's important to get up early with my children, get them dressed and eat breakfast together. She also reminded me to hold my children, tell them I love them, praise them when they do something good, and stick with a punishment once I have set it.

The most valuable thing I learned was that I needed to set aside time to spend with my children to give them the attention they craved. I didn't realize that children need attention in order to thrive.

Closer Than Ever

Francisco and I reconnected during Family Group, where we could vent in a productive manner, and in one-on-one sessions with my counselor. She helped us to understand the roles we had played in each other's lives and work out our differences without blame.

One Saturday near the end of my treatment, Francisco picked me up to take our children to the zoo. I was thrilled. I had always wanted to do that. I'll never forget the expressions on our children's faces while they looked at the animals. It felt incredible to me that we could experience such joy as a family.

Francisco grabbed my hand and looked at me and said, "I love you, babe." On that day, I knew we were going to be OK. Even though I could not undo the past, we still had a future.

'Can I Do It?'

The day I returned home, I was overfilled with joy but also terrified. So many thoughts went through my head, like, "What if I can't do it? What if my kids hate me? Am I going to be able to handle the stress without getting high?"

I had spent six months only with my daughter and in the safe, structured environment of the program. I feared that I wasn't ready for the real world.

A big moment for me came about a month after I returned home. My caseworker, Geneva Thomas, came by for our weekly visit and my 4 year old started acting up. First he threw a ball at her. Immediately, I got on him and told him to stand in the corner. He told me no and continued to throw things.

I knew he was just trying to get attention, so I decided to ignore him. But Geneva saw that I was getting frustrated. "You need to deal with him," she said.

The New Me

I picked my son up and told him to stand in the corner. He started to shout. Then I was so embarrassed. I wanted to yell at him, "What the hell is wrong with you? Why are you acting like this?"

But that was the old me. I told myself, "That isn't the kind of parent you want to be." So I sat down with him in the corner. I told him we were going to sit there until we calmed down.

It felt like a good solution to me, but Geneva explained that I was punishing myself by sitting there with him. I felt so frustrated and confused. How was I supposed to handle him? Even though it took a lot of work, I finally got my son to stand in time-out by himself.

In the past, moments like this would have overwhelmed me and I would've gotten high. Not this time, though. I'm learning to handle my kids.

Handling My Children

Now it's been 18 months since I came home from treatment. I feel good. I know how to build a foundation for my children. I am learning to handle their outbursts in a positive way and am reaching out to Francisco for support.

I'm so glad my social worker didn't just throw me out into the world when I was done with treatment. She stood by me while I got adjusted. She also helped my family move into a new apartment and gave us referrals for furniture, clothing and food. Even after my case was closed, she was there if I had a problem or question.

Francisco and I are closer than ever. We are able to communicate without fighting. I feel that we can make it through everything and our love will not fade.

I am also more confident about myself as a mother. Through a program called Exceptional Parents Unlimited, a child development expert comes and works with my children and me once a week. She brings games for the kids to play or comes up with projects for us to do together, like baking or making our own Christmas ornaments.

The activities we share help to strengthen the bond between my children and me. I feel so proud of myself that I'm learning and growing as a mother.

Rise

www.risemagazine.org

LEADER'S GUIDE:

Closer Than Ever by Sandra Evans
I'm learning how to handle my children.

DISCUSSION FOCUS:
Nurturing your children.

ACTIVITY GOAL:
Participants will understand how to communicate love and care to their children.

STORY SUMMARY

Sandra was neglected and abused as a child and used drugs to handle her painful experiences. When she became a mother, she felt depressed and fearful. Soon she turned to meth whenever she became overwhelmed by caring for her children.

In treatment, Sandra learned to connect with her children through eating together, activities, praise, saying "I love you," consistent discipline, hugs and holding. Her relationships with her husband and her children improved.

DISCUSSION GUIDE

GROUP INTRODUCTION: 10 minutes

Today we're going to talk about nurturing our children. Many parents are determined not to raise their children as they were raised, but are not sure how to help their children feel loved and cared for. Simple things like holding infants during feedings, hugging and soothing your children by holding them, following a daily schedule, eating together, planning family activities, praising good behavior, and being consistent with discipline can help you and your children feel close and safe.

- How do you feel about this topic?
- Do you have experiences related to this topic that you'd like to share before we get started?

READ AND DISCUSS STORY: 15 + 30 minutes

Read the story out loud as a group. Help participants recognize the writer's emotions and coping mechanisms and their own. Go back over important moments in the story and ask the participants about how they've handled similar experiences:

STORY MOMENT	DISCUSSION QUESTION
Sandra learns that children need attention.	What have you been surprised to learn about children since becoming a parent?
Sandra finds that keeping her children on a schedule is a form of nurturing.	How do you communicate to your children that they can count on you to take care of their daily needs?
Sandra spends more time holding and hugging her children and giving them attention and praise.	What little things help you and your children feel good about being together?
Sandra enjoys activities with her children.	What places and activites do you enjoy sharing with your children?
Parenting classes and one-on-one support help Sandra feel confident.	How does your confidence in yourself as a parent affect how you treat your children?

JOURNAL TIME: 15-30 minutes

By writing in their journals, participants can more deeply reflect on their own experiences. Hand out the "Journal Reflections" worksheet and give participants time to write. They can share their responses with the group or in pairs, or after the workshop with a peer, family member, therapist or other important person in their lives.

NAME: **DATE:**

JOURNAL REFLECTIONS: Closer Than Ever by Sandra Evans

It can be difficult to feel close and connected to your children when you're busy and tired, yet pushing your children away can also make their behavior worse, as they whine, act demanding, or misbehave to get your attention. Sandra learned to use firm discipline but also to hold, praise and spend time having fun with her children.

Take some time to reflect on your strengths as a parent and new ways that you could nurture your children.

1. What are some activities that you enjoy doing with your children?

2. What are some times each day when your children can count on having your attention?

3. What are some ways that you soothe your children when they are upset?

4. How do you show your children that you're proud of their behavior?

____

____

____

____

ACTION STEPS

Sandra finds that when she gets help with her fears, she's able to feel more connected to her children. Write down 2-3 ways that you could handle fears or frustrations that are making it difficult to feel close to your children.

1. ____

____

____

2. ____

____

____

3. ____

____

____

A SUPPORTIVE CONNECTION

I plan to get support and encouragement by talking about my reflections and action steps with:

____

Do Over

Changing as a parent takes courage and practice.

By Youshell Williams

Most parents like me want their children to have an easy, decent life as far removed from what we ourselves experienced as possible. We want to be good parents, but sometimes it can be very difficult to know how if you grew up in foster care or in a home where you experienced abuse or neglect.

Losing my children to the system made me realize that I had a lot to overcome from my past and a lot to change about my ways of thinking as a parent.

So, how do you become a terrific parent even if you didn't have one? That's a very good question. It's also the subtitle of The Whole Parent by therapist Debra Wesselmann. Her book helped me think about new ways to overcome my feelings of inadequacy so that I can change my life and my children's lives for the better. Here is her advice to parents:

It is a challenge to know how to give your child a secure nurturing environment if you grew up in the foster care system, especially if, like many children in care, you were shuttled between foster families or went back and forth between foster care and your birth home many times.

'Am I Good Enough?'

A person in that situation grows up not really having an idea what a healthy family life should look like, and often has lots of self-doubts like, "Why me? Why didn't my parents love me? Why didn't another family love me? Was I unlovable?" In truth, the system and the adults in our lives have let us down.

Experiences that lead you to doubt your self-worth can leave you feeling like you're not good enough when you start raising your own families. Sometimes the anger and pain on our children's faces during difficult moment just triggers all the shame and guilt and "I'm not good enough" feelings that parents feel inside.

One mother I worked with had a lot of traumatic experiences growing up. Her own mother died of alcoholism. Still, she has successfully raised three nice children. It's amazing what she's done, despite feeling at times that she wasn't good enough or lovable.

This mom found a good mate, a good supportive church environment, and supportive friends. She looked to other people who

(Continued on next page)

(Continued from previous page)
she admired as parents and tried to emulate them. So becoming a good parent even when you have grown up in foster care definitely can be done, but it's important to be conscious of the challenges you face and stay motivated.

Changing Angry Reactions

Another challenge for parents who had negative experiences as children is that early experiences are lodged in the emotional part of the brain, which creates responses that feel so automatic that your actions may not feel like something you can consciously control.

When parents respond to various things that their children do with negative responses that feel extreme and out of sync with how they want to treat their children, it's often very difficult for them to understand why they respond the way they do. But you can change those automatic responses with a lot of effort.

For example, I worked with a mom who was having strong angry reactions. In therapy, the mom realized that when her son was doing some typical teenage things, like rolling his eyes or not jumping to when she asked him to, she was getting a feeling that her son didn't love her. She was able to say, "Oh, it's the very same feeling I have when I'm around my mother. I feel rejected like I felt rejected as a child." That rejection feeling made her very angry.

Once the mom put that together, she started being able to recognize that her son's typical teen behaviors were not rejections, and she was able to deal with those feelings of hurt related to her upbringing.

Common Misperceptions

In The Whole Parent I talk about a number of other common parental misperceptions that relate to negative childhood experiences—like, "my child is invading me," or "my child is abusive," or "I have to have complete control for my child to be safe."

I worked with a father who was having strong rage reactions when his 7 year old would embarrass him in public. His immediate reaction was, "What are people thinking of me? They're thinking I'm a bad father and a terrible person," and he just wanted to kill his son. But as he worked through those feelings with me, he realized that growing up with an alcoholic father had left him feeling very insecure about the way people were looking at him, and this trauma was being tapped into.

That's not to say that we don't all feel embarrassed when our children act out in public, but we're being irrational if we begin to think, "I'm a bad person," or "People think I'm a bad person" and take those feelings out on the child, because every parent has had embarrassing incidents in public.

A Chance to Heal

The good news is that, when you realize the ways you're thinking and acting might be hurting you and your child, and you consciously set out to change your thoughts and behaviors, you can break those negative patterns. You can give your children much more positive feelings about themselves than you might have had.

One technique is to write out our irrational thoughts and feelings and then practice having different thoughts and feelings. The mother who felt rejected by her teenage son could write herself a little reminder card with her irrational feeling at the top: "My child is rejecting me." Underneath it she might write: "This is not true. All teenagers sometimes act like they don't have respect for their parents. I'm getting him confused with my mom. He's really not my mom. I love him and he loves me." And she could carry that reminder card with her and read it over and over until it really sinks in.

I often have people do writing exercises, such as writing down their irrational beliefs on one side of the paper, like, "My child is abusive" and writing down on other side some rational, logical responses they could have when those feelings come up.

Finding Support

You can also break negative patterns by getting help from a good support network. Whether you attend a support group or speak to a therapist, religious leader, a loving mate, or a supportive group of friends, you need people who you can talk to openly and honestly.

You can also find another parent who you admire who you can really talk to, and you can read books about the effects of trauma on parenting. Whatever way you choose, it's important to sort out how your past might be affecting the way you feel as a parent and take steps to change your thinking and behavior.

Working on your own childhood issues takes tremendous courage. It's a lot easier to try not to think about what you went through. It's painful to look back on abuse or neglect you faced as a child, but if you don't, your parenting will not get better. Parents can face the traumas of the past, recognize how those experiences are affecting them as parents, and make changes so their children will grow up safe and secure.

Breaking the Chain

Building a calm, safe home for my son.

By Evelyn Salazar

Translated from Spanish.

When my son Dylan was 2, his father and I separated. I had to confront the reality that we weren't coming together as parents, but instead were arguing and screaming at each other. At times he would even shove me or grab me by the arm.

It was very hard to make a decision to leave. I knew it would be sad for Dylan not to live with his father. But I also didn't want him to grow up watching us fight. I thought, "Is this the example I want to give him?"

Finding Support

I found a therapist, hoping she could help keep Dylan's father and me together, or help us communicate if we split up. But he wouldn't go.

After we split up, I decided to keep going to the therapist, Liza, at the Center for Family Life in Sunset Park. I knew that it would help me to get someone's support and have a place where I could unburden myself at a time when I was feeling so alone.

At that time, Dylan spoke only a little. He was very restless and seemed frustrated, I think because he wanted to express something that he couldn't say, or because it was hard for me to know what he wanted.

Liza suggested he go to a special school where he could get help with controlling his restlessness and anger, as well as other things he didn't feel comfortable doing, like painting and playing with sticky things (because he didn't like to get himself dirty or wet).

Really, I didn't think it was a big problem, but in the few months Dylan went to the school – Wow! I noticed that he was no longer so restless and didn't get angry over every little thing, and I could see his curiosity growing. He was maturing. It was very satisfying to see how he learned and grew.

Now Dylan is 4 years old, and he has distinguished himself as a very curious and playful child who likes to be amused and to get a lot of attention. He has a great imagination and is also very intelligent – he took that from me, ha ha ha.

Tender Moments

Sometimes Dylan is so tender, like when he comes home after being with his father. He opens the door and says, "Mami, I have a surprise for you! Close your eyes!"

When I open them he says, "I have a rose for you, the prettiest mother in the world, so you'll never be sad."

This fills me with tears and I throw myself down in front of his little body. (Other times, he says that he's my surprise!)

Sometimes Dylan asks me questions that I don't know the answers to, and couldn't imagine existed in his little head. He asks me what he was like when he was a baby, what it was like when he was in my stomach, how he was born, what his body was like then, what he could do and what he couldn't do.

He also asks things like, "Why do the leaves fall from the trees? Why is it cloudy?" Wow! I have to turn into a meteorologist to give him a satisfying answer.

Being Playful

Dylan especially likes to play pretend. He says to me, "Mami, we're going to play that you're Dora and I'm Boots, OK?"

"OK."

"Hello, Dora."

"Hello, Boots."

"What are you doing, Dora?"

"Nothing, Boots. I am walking home. And you, Boots?"

"Me too, Dora," and we go from there.

The funniest is when he says to me, "Mami, we're going have a conversation, OK?"

"Have a conversation about what?"

"About you, about me, everything, Mommy. Everything, OK?"

"OK."

"Start, Mami."

"You start!" and then we start to chat about whatever thing.

Putting Him First

At times things aren't easy because I'm tired and he wants to play. I say, "Play by yourself and later I'll play with you," but hardly five minutes will go by before he comes back to me.

Sometimes at night I want to go directly to bed but I have to put him to bed first, reading him a story and the whole procedure before he'll go to sleep. There are times when I'm reading his story and I fall asleep and he nudges me, saying, "Mami, wake up! Mami, don't sleep!"

I try to skip pages so we can get through it more quickly, but he'll catch me and say, "Oh, no, Mami, that's not how it goes, this is how..." and make me go back.

Dealing With Tantrums

Dylan also has a very strong character, like his father and me. If he doesn't get a lot of attention, he gets angry. When things don't go his way, he can throw tremendous tantrums. He cries furiously and has a very strong voice, so over his crying you can hear him screaming and screaming, and sometimes knocking things down. It's overwhelming.

I don't always know what reaction to have. It used to be that one of us would shout, and the other would shout back, and then we'd keep shouting, like a chain. I know now that I have to break that chain.

It's not easy. At times I feel a sense of desperation, but I try to keep communication going. I say, "Dylan, if you don't scream, I can understand you better. I know you're mad, but let's calmly try to resolve this situation."

When he has a tantrum in public, I just try not to feel ashamed if he makes a scene. I talk to him, or I fill myself with strength and count, "Two, three, four" minutes until he calms down.

I Try to Be Firm

I know that he needs to learn that when his mother says no, she means it. I don't want him thinking, "Oh, Mami says that but she'll change her mind." Although it's difficult to not give in to him, and to not be able to give him everything he wants, I try not to give in to his demands too much.

Sometimes when we're playing a game and I win, he gets mad and messes up the game, or he wants to play it again so he can win. If I won't play again, he cries and screams.

I try to be firm and to speak clearly, without starting to scream myself, saying, "Dylan, look at me, listen to me. I know you wanted to win, but one person can't always win. There's going to be times when it's your turn to lose. It's not a problem. You don't have to get angry."

Sometimes he keeps crying and I leave him. I say, "When you feel better, you tell me what you want." That works well. I don't give a lot of attention to his tantrum, and he calms down and talks to me.

A Stable Home

In the past two years, Dylan and I have learned a lot together. I pay more attention to him, and he does the same to me.

Although we don't live with his father, he sees him two days each week and every other weekend. Dylan has told me that he would like for all three of us to be together. I had to explain to him, "Papi has his house, and Mami has her own. But the important thing is that although we're separate, we're content."

Now Dylan has security and stability at home. When his father and I were together we had an unstable relationship, with one person running one way and the other running in the opposite direction. I think Dylan saw that and didn't know what to think, or just got sad seeing his parents disoriented and upset.

Dylan's father is a friend to me now. We're both striving to stay calm and do the best for our child.

My Great Satisfaction

Becoming a mother has given me more responsibility and I have matured. I've had to analyze who I am and how to get the results that I want for myself and my son.

If I get mad or frustrated, I try to understand why I'm reacting that way and to ask myself, "What's the best way I can handle this situation?" In the past I responded like a lion, or I just wanted to run away. Now I respond like a cat, and I stay and find a solution.

It's a great feeling of satisfaction to look at my son and see him growing. When he achieves something, I know that I am a big part of that. That's fantastic! I let myself heave a great sigh, a great love from very deep down in my heart.

Rise

www.risemagazine.org

LEADER'S GUIDE:

Breaking the Chain by Evelyn Salazar
Building a calm, safe home for my son.

DISCUSSION FOCUS:
Connecting through play.

ACTIVITY GOAL:
Participants will recognize the activities and games that they enjoy doing with their children.

STORY SUMMARY

Evelyn's son, Dylan, has a strong personality, like his mother. Sometimes he delights Evelyn with his thoughtfulness and curiosity. Other times he overwhelms her with his demands and temper tantrums.

Evelyn shows how playing with her son has brought them closer and helped Dylan to grow. She also shows how she tries to be firm when he has tantrums, encouraging him to use words to express how he feels instead of actions.

DISCUSSION GUIDE

GROUP INTRODUCTION: 10 minutes

Today we're going to talk about the importance of playing. It's important that your child has plenty of time to play with friends, play alone, and play with you. Play helps children learn how to get along with others and negotiate. It improves their ability to use words (instead of negative behavior) to express themselves. Playing with your child can also help you have a closer relationship with your child – good times that balance out the times when you make demands on your child or you must be apart.

- How do you feel about this topic?
- Do you have experiences related to this topic that you'd like to share before we get started?

READ AND DISCUSS STORY: 15 + 30 minutes

Read the story out loud as a group. Help participants recognize the writer's emotions and coping mechanisms and their own. Go back over important moments in the story and ask the participants about how they've handled similar experiences:

STORY MOMENT	DISCUSSION QUESTION
Evelyn describes different ways of playing and interacting with her son: Answering his questions, playing pretend, reading stories.	What games or activities do your children like to play with you?
Dylan learns to express his thoughts and feelings with words by playing at having a conversation.	What do you think your children learn by playing?
Playing together is helping Dylan learn to better tolerate frustration, like the frustration he feels when he loses a game.	How do you think play can help your children learn to handle frustration?
At times, Evelyn feels open to playing and at other times she is tired, busy or does not want to play.	How do you respond most times that your children want to play?
Evelyn says that playing together has brought her and Dylan closer: "I pay more attention to him and he does the same to me."	How do you see your relationship with your child being affected when you and your child play together, or when you don't have time to play as much?

JOURNAL TIME: 15-30 minutes

By writing in their journals, participants can more deeply reflect on their experiences and the steps they can take to strengthen themselves and their families. Hand out the "Journal Reflections" worksheet and give participants 15-30 minutes to write. They can share their responses with the group or in pairs, or after the workshop with a counselor, therapist, or peer.

NAME: **DATE:**

JOURNAL REFLECTIONS: Breaking the Chain by Evelyn Salazar

Evelyn sees that the games she plays with her son are helping him use words to express his feelings, handle negative feelings like frustration, and express his thoughts through imaginary play.

Take some time to reflect on what your children can learn and express through play and how you can bring more playtime into your lives. Use the questions below to guide your reflections.

1. What games and activities do you enjoy playing with your child—or might you enjoy?

---

2. How do you feel when you're playing together?

---

3. What concerns do you have about the way your child plays?

---

4. What gets in the way of enjoying playtime with your children?

ACTION STEPS

Setting aside time to play with your child and creating an area at home where your child can play freely can help your child handle stress and develop and grow. Write 2-3 steps you could take to bring more playtime into your lives.

1.

2.

3.

A SUPPORTIVE CONNECTION

I plan to get support and encouragement by talking about my reflections and action steps with:

'One Child Felt Like One Thousand'

Better communication helped my son and me handle his ADHD.

By Ilka Perez

What is ADHD? A few years ago I had no idea what that stood for (Attention Deficit Disorder with Hyperactivity) and had never heard of it. But I found out I had a beautiful little boy dealing with it.

Some days Alex was fine, what you might call a normal boy. Most days were hectic. One child felt like one thousand. He was all over the place, starting one thing and never finishing, just jumping to the next.

There were times when Alex would cry for no reason. In school, he would pick up objects and hit other children, just out of the blue. Once we were at a hair salon and he decided to hit the neon light with a key chain until it broke. Not only did I have to pay the owner back, but sitting there, I could have sworn I heard what people were thinking: "She has no control over that child." I couldn't understand why he would do such a thing.

Alex was about 4 then. I knew that for his age, certain behaviors were not normal. I was completely convinced something was wrong and when he cried I did too. We were both frustrated, upset, confused and lost.

Determined to Find Help

I was convinced it was my fault. Alex was my first child and I was young and scared. This was my first time ever dealing with a little human being. I thought, "Did I do something wrong? Am I forgetting some type of motherly love? Maybe I'm not spending enough time with him, or someone hurt him and he doesn't know how to tell me."

I had to get him help. I told my son's doctor, "Alex cries for no reason, he can't stay still at all. He's been aggressive in class." I was afraid that I would be looked at as a crazy person, but the doctor told me Alex had ADHD. He said I was not the only parent dealing with this problem, and there was help.

I was relieved to know there was a name for what was controlling my son and upsetting me. I was determined to find help.

Searching for Options

Unfortunately, every doctor wanted to dig a pill down my child's throat. The medication they wanted Alex to take sounded very scary. I kept thinking, "What if there are long-term side affects?" That wasn't the treatment I wanted for my child.

Instead of a pill that my son would grow dependent on, or that would cause other problems, I wanted to really understand what his little innocent mind was going through and why he was feeling the way he was.

I needed information. I started educating myself about ADHD by reading books, going on the Internet and picking up some booklets at the hospital.

Finally I met a doctor who listened to me. She met with us a few times and took time to talk with Alex in a playful way. She spoke to him about things he was interested in, like cartoons and certain toys that were in style, and played with some toys with him. Alex enjoyed her company.

When she put all her focus on Alex, it was like he let her in his mind for a moment. Alex was very open to her questions and responded with excitement, telling her everything in his imagination as if he was talking to another child. We both noticed he was very bright, curious and talkative when he was comfortable.

Information and Support

The doctor explained all the options-further testing, medication, support groups (for me) and family therapy. She also suggested some reading material to me, which was very helpful. It gave tips on how to talk to him and how to understand his actions. For instance, I found out that children with ADHD need you to make a lot of eye contact in order to get their full attention, and they constantly need praise to encourage their good behavior.

I had a clear view of the treatment I wanted for Alex. By attending play therapy weekly with me, I knew that he could improve his focus and grow a longer attention span. So I made a definite decision that Alex would not take any medication, not even a taste.

Instead, I searched for play therapy sessions. The material the doctor had given me included some phone numbers of organizations that held meetings for parents of children with ADHD. I started with that, and then asked around in my neighborhood.

It took a while, and lot of disappointments, but finally I found the Center for Family Life in Sunset Park, and it was a success. Attending therapy at the Center has helped Alex remarkably.

'Hear Your Child Out'

By the time I entered those doors, I was exhausted from searching but I felt good about this place. Meeting the therapist, Melissa, was amazing. She was young, and her room was bright and not a drag-it was filled with toys and felt like home, not a doctor's office.

She got to understand Alex by meeting with me first. We spoke about his history, what he likes and doesn't like, and what changes I would like to see in my son. Then she started meeting with Alex and me.

Right away I saw changes in Alex. In her office, he was outspoken with his opinions. He would walk through her room and tell Melissa what he wanted to do that day.

Before we went to family therapy, I saw him as just a child who couldn't understand the adult world. I treated him almost like he would never get older or grow up, so I didn't pay close attention to what he said or to the signs of how he was developing.

Melissa showed me how important it is to hear a child out, to really try to understand what children are expressing, even if they're just crying, and to explain things to your child. When I started listening to Alex closely, I realized that he's his own person trying to understand the world, and that I can prepare him to make decisions of his own one day.

A Big Change

Melissa gave me so many techniques to try with Alex. She recommended I keep a calendar for Alex and me so he would know ahead of time when I would work and when he would see Melissa. At first it didn't work, maybe because he was too little or because my schedule kept changing, but it does now. I tell Alex when I work and who will pick him up from school.

Being a first time mother, I was overwhelmed with all the information and a lot of it took a long time to fully understand. But Alex is the most important thing in my life and getting him the right treatment was very important to me.

After we spent a year and a half getting really close to Melissa, she told me that she was leaving the Center because she was pregnant. I was in shock. Once again I felt lost and alone. I also feared that Alex wouldn't understand.

We decided to tell him in a very cheerful manner, saying, "Melissa is having a baby and now she has to take care of the baby." Alex didn't really show any expression but he wondered who the new therapist would be.

I thought that Alex would have a hard time with this new transition but he took it very well. When we met Jill, it was like we knew her already. In some ways she was hipper, more like Alex, and he took a liking to her right away.

Alex is now 8 years old and still loves visiting Jill. He looks forward to all the activities she has in mind for him. Best of all, I get to meet with her, too.

Sticking to Routine

Jill gives Alex choices and gives him the opportunity to share his opinions or just what is on his mind. I now plan his day so his mind doesn't have to wander and worry. Sticking to a routine-just basics like getting up at the same time in the morning, getting ready for school, knowing what to expect after school and what things need to get done-helps him stay calm and focused. Alex now knows how to start something and finish, even if that means Mom has to remind him.

What I enjoy most is speaking to him and hearing how his day was in school or what happened between his friends. His imagination is the most precious thing.

Treatment Helped My Son and Me

When I looked to the doctors for help, I was overwhelmed. The doctors spoke to me as if I was a child. I guess because I was a young mother they assumed I wouldn't understand. They wanted to tell me what to do without explaining all the options.

I'm glad I stood up for myself and dug up information about my son's condition on my own. Understanding ADHD better gave me the confidence to ask the doctors tougher questions, and led me to treatment that's helped my son and me.

Jill and I found a solution for Alex-we used his hyperactivity for positive things. With her help, I have seen Alex change a lot. Sometimes I smiled, other days I cried, feeling like I didn't even know my child, like there was some blockage between us. There was: ADHD.

Now there is no longer a blockage between us because we have learned how to live comfortably with each other. Alex will always have to battle ADHD but now we both know how to deal with it.

Rise

www.risemagazine.org

LEADER'S GUIDE:

One Child Felt Like One Thousand by Ilka Perez

Family therapy helped my son and me handle his ADHD.

DISCUSSION FOCUS:

Communicating with your child.

ACTIVITY GOAL:

Participants will understand how improved communication can reduce children's acting out behavior.

STORY SUMMARY

Ilka writes about her journey to find help for herself and her son, who has ADHD (Attention Deficit Hyperactivity Disorder). Ilka searches for good information about ADHD, a condition that can make it harder for children to stay focused and calm. With the help of family therapy, Ilka works to understand her son and to create structures in his day and week to help him remain in control and feeling good about himself.

DISCUSSION GUIDE

GROUP INTRODUCTION: 10 minutes

Today we're going to talk about communicating with our children. Many parents underestimate what children can understand and what children need to know to feel safe and in control of their lives. Explaining what children can expect to do each day or from each activity can help even very young children feel comfortable and behave well. Parents can also underestimate how much children are trying to communicate their needs. Listening to your child's needs can prevent tantrums and conflicts.

- How do you feel about this topic?
- Do you have experiences related to this topic that you'd like to share before we get started?

READ AND DISCUSS STORY: 15 + 30 minutes

Read the story out loud as a group. Help participants recognize the writer's emotions and coping mechanisms and their own. Go back over important moments in the story and ask the participants about how they've handled similar experiences:

STORY MOMENT	DISCUSSION QUESTION
Ilka goes to a family therapist who says it's important to explain things to a child, like the daily routine.	How do you explain daily routines or changes in the routine to your child?
Ilka writes, "I treated my son almost like he would never grow up, so I didn't pay close attention to what he said."	How does your child show you his needs, frustration or concerns?
Ilka learns that better communicate can help reduce children's tantrums or acting out behavior.	How might you prepare your children for new experiences or use communication to avoid a conflict?
Being busy or stressed can make it more difficult to take time to know or listen to your children.	What is getting in the way of communicating with your child now?
Ilka communicates more with her son and sees that he has improved his ability to start and finish a task.	How have you seen changes in your children (positive and negative) when you've made changes in your family life?

JOURNAL TIME: 15-30 minutes

By writing in their journals, participants can more deeply reflect on their experiences and the steps they can take to strengthen themselves and their families. Hand out the "Journal Reflections" worksheet and give participants 15-30 minutes to write. They can share their responses with the group or in pairs, or after the workshop with a counselor, therapist, or peer.

NAME: **DATE:**

JOURNAL REFLECTIONS: One Child Felt Like 1000 by Ilka Perez

By attending family therapy with her son, Ilka learns that when her son is better prepared for daily tasks, he's more able to behave well, complete tasks and handle changes in his routines.

Take some time to think over how you communicate with your child and how you could improve communication in your family. Use the questions below to guide your reflections.

1. How do talk with your children about what they can expect from each day, especially changes in the daily routine?

2. How do you make time to listen to your children's daily experiences?

3. How do your children express their needs or feelings with behavior instead of with words?

4. How do you prepare your children for new or difficult experiences, like starting school or staying with a new babysitter?

ACTION STEPS

What behaviors do you think you could help your children change by communicating with them more? Write down 2-3 steps you could take to improve how you listen to and talk with your children.

1.

2.

3.

A SUPPORTIVE CONNECTION

I plan to get support and encouragement by talking about my reflections and action steps with:

Education Starts at Home

My children need my support to succeed in school.

By Maribel Martinez

Translated from Spanish

When I was growing up in Mexico, my mother always paid attention to my education. She worked in a store that we had in the house. If we had a problem in the school, my mother simply closed the store without regard to whether she would lose money and went to the school to talk with our teacher.

My mother never said to us, "I had to close the store and I lost money," or, "Today I can't go speak to your teacher." My mother told us that school was the most important thing for us, and that what we learned, nobody could take from our hands.

My Broken Dreams

I had dreams for my own education. I thought I'd graduate high school, even though that would be difficult because of our economic situation. Despite having to pay for school fees, uniforms and books, I finished secondary school (8th grade here).

I took my exam to apply to high school and found a part-time job as a receptionist so I'd be able to cover my high school expenses. But then my mother decided that we should move to the United States to improve our financial situation.

I was 14 when we arrived here. Living in New York was much more difficult than my mother had thought. In Mexico, we didn't pay rent because we owned a home. Here, we had to pay rent. Food, telephone, gas, and lights were all so expensive. I had to go straight to work.
Investing in My Children

We thought we'd save money so that when we went back to Mexico, I could return to school. But nothing went as we had hoped. Eventually, I had my children and I never went back home.

Now, as a mother of three students, I worry about how they are doing in school. I hope that my children can complete their education and achieve a career that they really feel a passion for and enjoy.

Before my children started school, I taught them the numbers, colors and the alphabet, as well as songs, animal sounds and the names of many things. It was funny, because when they were learning numbers, we'd go outside and count the trees, cars, houses, birds, planes, everything!

An Educational Schedule

I am lucky to have a schedule at my job that allows me to remain very involved in my children's education. I work 8:30 to 2:30, and that allows me to pick up my children or wait for them at home. Since they don't like the school food, I cook something quickly and at 3:30 we eat together.

We talk about how their day went and if they had any difficulties in class. We listen to each other, although at times we all want to talk at the same time.

In these conversations, I find out their favorite subjects and those they don't enjoy. My daughter Gabriela doesn't like science. She'll say, "Mami, today I had science," and make a face.

Liliana doesn't enjoy math. She tells me, "I need help, Mami. I need the whole world to help me."

Fernando always says that he's fine, just that at times his teacher gives him a detention–he says it's because some kids made noise and the whole class got punished.

We have a schedule. At 4:30 we start homework. Sometimes Fernando puts on his headphones and reads, and that allows the rest of us to work quietly. I clean up the kitchen and check with them to see if they need my help.
Homework Help

Even though I don't speak much English, I am very involved in my children's homework. I help them find words in the dictionary, organize their papers and notebooks, and read alongside them.

We've found ways for me to help them with school and for them to get the help I can't give them. Often my children translate assignments or questions that they're confused by, and I help them in Spanish.

Recently Gabriela she was having trouble in math and her siblings weren't able to help her. Fernando translated the problem for me, and I explained it, and he translated back to English, but Gabriela said, "You don't know anything! I'm going to call the hotline number."

She'd seen on TV that New York City has a homework help line that children and families can call. When she got off the phone, she said, "They said the same thing you said…I only wanted to be sure!" But now, we are always calling that phone number.

I Wish I Spoke English

Fernando, who is in the 6th grade, often stays after school and asks a teacher to help him with his homework. Liliana, who is in the 7th grade, often helps her younger siblings learn.

When my children are doing homework in English and I don't understand anything, I sometimes feel bad. I know I should speak better English and I worry that I have to go back to school if I want to help my children succeed.

Four years ago I took a class and earned my GED in Spanish. I also answered 100 questions in English and received a diploma in English, too. Step by step, I hope I will find opportunities to further my studies, and I study English a little at home now.

'You're Super-Intelligent!'

In New York, children in some grades take citywide tests they must pass to pass the grade. My children get nervous about a week before the citywide tests. But I don't feel nervous because I talk with the teachers and I know my children are well prepared.

When my children feel nervous, I tell them, "You can do it. Haven't you done the homework? Haven't you gone to school?"

"Yes," they say.

"Then you're going to pass the grade! You're super-intelligent!"

At my children's schools, the teachers also tell parents how they can help their children at home, such as by listening to them read or reading to them for half an hour every day. Although many parents work long hours, we all have half an hour before our children go to bed when we could read.

Involved at School

Whenever I can, I help at my children's school. When the school year starts, I go to the school to meet my children's new teacher and to find out her daily routine, how much homework she assigns, what tests she gives, and what she expects in terms of class participation.

I think it's so important that parents help and support our children with their schoolwork. Discipline and education start at home. What makes me feel disappointed and angry is that very few parents seem to attend meetings with teachers or take part in school activities.

One day I received an invitation to attend a breakfast with the principal where parents could discuss their concerns. Only 10 parents out of about 800 students showed up! I know that many parents work during the day and can't attend meetings, but I had spoken to some mothers who had concerns and could've come but didn't. I was frustrated.

There was coffee and cake spread out and the principal was waiting for more people to come. "Where are the other mothers?" I thought. Finally, we just got started.

My Voice Was Heard

The principal introduced herself and asked us each to say our name and what brought us to the meeting.

When it was my turn, I said, "As you know, my daughter's teacher is pregnant. Many of the mothers are concerned about who might be replacing her and whether the new teacher will know where to begin." Our children were in the 3rd grade and had to pass the citywide exam at the end of the year. Children's third grade teachers are really important!

I continued, saying, "The children love their teacher and are used to how she teaches. We're concerned about how switching to a substitute might affect them. My suggestion is that the substitute could start at least a week before the teacher leaves, so that she's integrated into the classroom, and our children don't feel such a big change and can focus on preparing for the test."

"That sounds to me like a good idea. If the teachers work together, the children won't be as affected. Thank you for your idea and your support," the principal said.

When I left the school I felt calm. I felt that the principal had heard my concerns

Education Starts at Home

I feel that the more we're involved as parents, the better our children will be as students. Although all of us are busy, the connection we make with our children's schools is important. If we can all just do a little, our children will feel more supported in pursuing their education and secure that they can achieve in school.

I've learned from supporting my children that the way they teach now is completely different from the way I was taught when I was little. They're expected to speak up in class and to ask questions, while I was expected to memorize what I was told. I can help them better when I understand more about what their teachers expect of them.

My children understand that their education is important to me and will give them a brilliant future. They see that they can have a job that they enjoy. They see that their teachers can own a car and a house and can go out and travel. This fascinates them. Those aren't options for our family.

My children are good students not only because I talk to them about the importance of school, but because I study alongside them and I show them that their schools are worth my time.

Rise

www.risemagazine.org

LEADER'S GUIDE:

Education Starts at Home by Maribel Martinez

My children need my support to succeed in school.

DISCUSSION FOCUS:

Setting up home routines and structures.

ACTIVITY GOAL:

Participants will identify the routines that could make their parenting more predictable.

STORY SUMMARY

Maribel grew up in Mexico and was unable to finish school because of her family's economic circumstances. Although she doesn't speak English and cannot always help her children understand their homework, Maribel supports her children's achievement in school by attending school meetings, creating time at home to talk about school and homework, and studying alongside her children. Maribel has created a safe, predictable home where her children feel supported in school achievement.

DISCUSSION GUIDE

GROUP INTRODUCTION: 10 minutes

Today we're going to talk about how predictable routines—like bathtimes and bedtimes, mealtimes, and homework time—can help children feel good and behave well. Children like their home environments to be as predictable as possible. They tend to act out when they're not sure what's expected of them. Parenting is easier if you get children dressed and ready in the same way each morning, do homework and eat meals at the same time each day, and get children ready for bedtime with calm activities like a bath and reading. Routines can help your children thrive at home and in school.

- How do you feel about this topic?
- Do you have experiences related to this topic that you'd like to share before we get started?

READ AND DISCUSS STORY: 15 + 30 minutes

Read the story out loud as a group. Help participants recognize the writer's emotions and coping mechanisms and their own. Go back over important moments in the story and ask the participants about how they've handled similar experiences:

STORY MOMENT	DISCUSSION QUESTION
Maribel has created routines that support her goal to help her children succeed in school.	What are your goals for your children?
Maribel eats and talks with her children after school each day.	How do you create routines to help your children achieve your goals for them?
After eating, Maribel's children do their homework.	How do you create special times for important things like homework, chores or bedtime?
Maribel has organized her work time to accommodate her family time.	What barriers do you face in setting up routines for your family?
Though she is a single mother of three, Maribel describes a calm, orderly household.	How would you like to bring more order to your family life?

JOURNAL TIME: 15-30 minutes

By writing in their journals, participants can more deeply reflect on their experiences and the steps they can take to strengthen themselves and their families. Hand out the "Journal Reflections" worksheet and give participants 15-30 minutes to write. They can share their responses with the group or in pairs, or after the workshop with a counselor, therapist, or peer.

NAME: **DATE:**

JOURNAL REFLECTIONS: Education Starts at Home by Maribel Martinez

In general, daily routines help children feel calm and safe. Maribel's goal as a parent is to set up a home life that will help her children succeed in school.

Take some time to reflect on how you can set up your home life to help your children behave well and succeed in reaching their goals and yours. Use the questions below to guide your reflections.

1. What is one routine that you consistently follow in your home?

2. How do you help your children get ready in the morning, go to bed at night, bathe themselves, or clean up the house?

3. How do you see your children's behavior change when your family goes through times of stress and chaos?

4. How do you help your family get back on track after disruptions?

ACTION STEPS

Many parents do not follow as many set routines with their children as they could. Write down 2-3 steps you could take to establish routines that could make your day go more smoothly.

1.

2.

3.

A SUPPORTIVE CONNECTION

I plan to get support and encouragement by talking about my reflections and action steps with:

Not a Baby Anymore

My daughter's tantrums were a sign that I needed to let her grow up.

By Sylvia Perez

My daughter, Lydia, had some very serious problems when she started the second grade. School was never too smooth for her, so on the first day this year I was encouraging her, saying, "This year is a new year for you." I had high hopes.

A Difficult First Day

I dressed Lydia in her uniform—yellow tights with a blue jumper and a long sleeve yellow shirt. She didn't want to put on her blue tie. But we came to an agreement. As we approached the school, Lydia started crying, holding on to a metal railing and refusing to go inside. "It'll be OK," I told her. "You look so beautiful."

In the cafeteria where the noise was tremendous and everyone's moms and dads were looking for the new teachers, quite a few children were crying, so I didn't feel as bad that my baby was in tears.

Her teacher, Ms. Thomas, had short black hair and looked very quiet. I knew by her gentle face that Lydia would like her. Ms. Thomas told me I could walk her upstairs to the classroom. Lydia did not let go of my hand, but when she picked out a desk, Lydia finally calmed down and I gave her a last kiss goodbye.

'I Will Behave'

But Lydia's fears did not go away as the year went on. She was having a major problem dealing with the other kids, especially two boys who she said called her "stupid" and "chicken leg." And she kept crying and not respecting the teacher's rules. Her attitude seemed to be that she ran the show. I was embarrassed when I heard about her behavior.

The teacher began calling to say Lydia was throwing herself on the floor and not doing her work, poking kids with her pencil and threatening kids with scissors. That was very scary. My husband and I were very upset. We took everything fun out of her room and made her write in her punishment book, "I will behave."

It didn't help. Soon the school counselor was calling me to say that Lydia's attitude was not good. She was always fidgeting and not in her seat. In about three weeks the school called at least six times and we had four conferences with the school counselor, principal, parent coordinator and teacher to discuss Lydia's behavior.

I blamed myself because soon after Lydia was born I relapsed (I had been addicted to drugs for many years). Because of my drug use, Lydia spent three years in foster care. But I also felt angry at Lydia. I felt she could do better and I didn't raise her to misbehave.

She Needed Help

In our house, everyone felt full with anger and disappointment. I felt stressed out and lost.

Lydia was getting so angry sometimes she would kick the wall, throw her toys everywhere in her room, tear things up, and do other destructive behaviors like that. She would even tell me she wished she was dead and she hated herself. She needed help.

I decided to call a mental health hotline. Because of her anger, her self-destructive behavior and her history in foster care, they advised me to take her to the emergency room so she could get a psychiatric evaluation.

When Lydia and I got there, we were sent to the adult psychiatric ward. I felt nervous for our safety. Everybody was in pajamas and some of the men seemed drunk or were talking to themselves. When we sat down, they all stared at us, especially Lydia in her braids and pink jacket. Immediately, she started crying and said she wanted to go home. She told me she would behave in school.

"I'm sorry, but this is what we need to do because you need help. You need to see a doctor," I told Lydia.

Earning Stars and Rewards

Finally, we met with a psychiatrist who advised us to start therapy and introduced us to a very nice therapist. I explained Lydia's behavior and the therapist said it sounds like she's having separation anxiety, probably because of her experience in foster care.

The therapist told me not to punish Lydia as much for her negative behavior but to reward her more for her positive behavior. By focusing on the positive things she does and encouraging her to do good, we can help Lydia feel better about herself and less fearful, frustrated and angry.

The therapist gave me a chart where Lydia can earn stars for the positive things she does. At the end of the week, if she has enough stars, she can earn a reward.

'Not a Baby Anymore'

The child psychologist also noticed me calling Lydia "Little Mama."

"Why are you doing that?" she asked.

"It's just something I call her," I said.

"No, Mom, do not do that," the psychologist said. "Mom, you need to call her Lydia. She's not little anymore, and she's the child."

"Ever since she was a baby I called her that. That's just how it has always been," I protested. But I said I would try.

She also told me I need to let Lydia grow up in certain ways. I have to stop getting her dressed, tying her shoes and cleaning her room. That is a tremendous change for us. "Treating her like a baby allows her to act like a baby," she said, "and that's part of why she has tantrums."

Playing Catch Up

The next morning when I took Lydia to school, I stopped by the parent coordinator's office. "Little Mama will be starting therapy," I told her.

Like the therapist, she politely asked me to stop calling her Mama. "When you do that, you're treating her like a baby. She's a big girl!"

That advice made me feel sad. I know she's a big girl, and I don't want to hurt her development in any way. But I also fear that her growing up is coming too soon. I feel that I missed out on Lydia's early years, so treating her like she is still small is a comfort for me. When I hug and kiss her, dress her and wipe her tears away, I feel like I'm playing catch up.

I Want to Protect Her

Plus, my own growing up was so terrible that I want to protect Lydia and keep her by my side always. I was only 5 years old when my mom and dad left my brothers and me alone in the streets. In my adoptive home, I was abused and beaten. I never had a birthday party or person who hugged me or truly loved me.

I suffered so much hoping all my life to see my mom again. When I was a teenager, I ran away looking for her. I needed a mother so bad. Even today I still feel like I need my parents. I wish I had a mother to love me and to help me raise my daughter. I wish I had my dad to hold on to me and protect me and let me know everything is going to be all right.

I love holding Lydia's hand as we walk and just being with her, letting her know I will always be here. I truly feel empty from my childhood and I don't want her to feel empty or alone.

Making Progress

Over the last month, Lydia and I have both been trying hard to follow the therapist's advice. Lydia goes to therapy every week and talks about being in foster care, missing her brothers, her fears about school, and her progress at school and at home.

We have a chart for the house activities and her teacher also has a chart with stars so we can see her progress at school. Everyone at the school is seeing how the therapy sessions and the charts are helping her. The teachers are giving me positive feedback

In the house Lydia is doing so well. She now makes her bed and cleans her room. She usually respects Mom and Dad and does her homework with no attitude. In the morning, she gets herself dressed for school and ties her shoes. Every night she reads at bedtime with me. I am so proud of her and I always tell her that with hugs and kisses.

There are days when she doesn't do what she's supposed to, like listening to the teacher or doing her work in class. Some days I feel a constant guilt that she's having problems. I think to myself, "If I didn't abandon her she would be different."

But I am beginning to see that Lydia and I can still be close as she gains more independence, and I feel proud of how much we've accomplished together. Little Mama—I mean Lydia—is growing up.

Rise

www.risemagazine.org

LEADER'S GUIDE:

Not a Baby Anymore by Sylvia Perez

My daughter's tantrums were a sign that I needed to let her grow up.

DISCUSSION FOCUS:

Helping your child become more independent.

ACTIVITY GOAL:

Participants will identify safe and positive ways to foster children's independence.

STORY SUMMARY

When Sylvia's daughter, Lydia, begins second grade, she is afraid of becoming more independent of her mother. Lydia doesn't want to go to school and she behaves badly in classes, hitting other children and throwing temper tantrums. With help from the school and a therapist, Sylvia learns that she contributes to her daughter's fears and behavior by treating Lydia like a baby.

Sylvia begins to allow Lydia more responsibilities at home and rewards Lydia for meeting her expectations. Over time, her behavior improves.

DISCUSSION GUIDE

GROUP INTRODUCTION: 10 minutes

Today we'll talk about children's need for independence and the struggles parents and children face as they try to figure out an appropriate level of independence for children of different ages. When children have too much freedom or not enough, they may act out in school or at home. Children may act out if they are feeling insecure, unconfident, confused, or angry, or if they believe that by creating and escalating a conflict, they can get their parent to give in. Setting clear expectations and showing children that you trust them to grow up can help children feel confident about themselves.

- How do you feel about this topic?
- Do you have experiences related to this topic that you'd like to share before we get started?

READ AND DISCUSS STORY: 15 + 30 minutes

Read the story out loud as a group. Help participants recognize the writer's emotions and coping mechanisms and their own. Go back over important moments in the story and ask the participants about how they've handled similar experiences:

STORY MOMENT	DISCUSSION QUESTION
Sylvia's daughter threw temper tantrums in school and fought with other kids.	What different emotions was Lydia expressing through her behavior?
Sylvia feels overwhelmed, guilty and angry about Lydia's behavior.	How have you felt when your children were acting out in public or at home?
Sylvia reacts by punishing Lydia but the therapist later tells her not to do that.	Why do you think punishment wasn't helping Lydia? What do you think of the therapist's advice?
Sylvia makes her expectations clear (with a chart) and rewards her daughter's good behavior.	How do you reward your children for good behavior?
Sylvia shows Lydia that it's OK to grow up.	How can you help your children feel confident about their ability to behave well in school or at home?

JOURNAL TIME: 15-30 minutes

By writing in their journals, participants can more deeply reflect on their own experiences. Hand out the "Journal Reflections" worksheet and give participants 15-20 minutes to write. They can share their responses with the group or in pairs, or after the workshop with a peer, family member, therapist or other important person in their lives.

NAME: **DATE:**

JOURNAL REFLECTIONS: Not a Baby Anymore by Sylvia Perez

When Sylvia's daughter had trouble behaving in school, Sylvia learned that she was giving her a daughter mixed messages about her behavior. On the one hand, she expected her to act her age and behave well in school. On the other, she treated her like a baby at home. Sylvia learned that she needed to make her expectations clear and reward positive behavior.

Take some time to reflect on how can you help your children feel confident about growing up.

In what ways does your child seem eager to grow up and in what ways does your child seem fearful?

What fears do you have about your child becoming more independent?

How do you communicate to your child that he or she can handle new responsibilities?

How do you reward your child for becoming more independent?

____

____

____

____

ACTION STEPS

It can be scary for children and parents to trust children to grow up. Write down 2-3 steps you could take to communicate your expectations and reward your children for becoming independent.

1. ____

____

____

2. ____

____

____

3. ____

____

____

A SUPPORTIVE CONNECTION

I plan to get support and encouragement by talking about my reflections and action steps with:

____

'What Can I Do?'

My children needed me to try new ways to parent.

By Latonya Baskerville

When my children first came home from foster care, life was different for all of us. I was clean and sober, thrown into a new apartment with three little strangers. My children were 10 years, 5 years and 2 weeks old when they were removed and 12, 7 and 18 months when they were returned.

Old-School Techniques

I was very confused about how to parent my children at first. The fact is, during my children's early years I used the parenting style I learned from family members. You know the model: beat your children if they disobey you, beat them if they talk back, beat them if they get in trouble, steal, have sex at a young age, act disrespectful. Beat them!

Don't get me wrong, some of the old school techniques are good and important. For example: have manners, be polite, respect your elders—that's a must. My children and grandchildren abide by these rules. But techniques like, "Children should be seen and not heard" and beating or controlling your children had to go.

I wonder where this method originated. My theory is that, for my community, it began with slavery. Parents probably figured that if they beat their own children, their masters wouldn't, and this would save the children's lives. The method was meant to protect children.

But beating your child doesn't really work. It creates silent and enraged children. These children grow up to be abusive adults, rigid and insensitive to their own children's feelings and needs.

I Needed to Change

Once I took parenting classes, I realized that the model I mimicked was not legal. If I wanted to keep my children out of foster care, I needed to change my style.

I told my children. "I really want to stop yelling and spanking. I've learned a new way to parent and this is the way we were going to live." We all agreed. We created new house rules, we rotated chores every month, and had family meetings regularly.

I also put up neon behavior charts. If my kids followed house rules, I rewarded them every pay period. If not, I rewarded myself. My children soon realized that I wouldn't yell and scream anymore when they didn't do their chores or when they misbehaved at school or at home. I would just go shopping.

Running Wild

But my children came home angry. For real, they were going crazy for two or three years.

When my teenage son started running wild, I didn't know how to respond. My son was having many problems at school, at home and in our neighborhood. He started getting high and gang banging. I thought I was going to bury my son before he was 18 years old.

I was so afraid of disciplining him the old way, but all I knew how to do was yell at him. We were arguing and cursing all the time. Our relationship was crazy.

'What Can I Do?'

Then came a knock on the door: A detective from the local precinct came at 2 a.m., holding a manila folder as thick as a cinder block. The detective had evidence that my son had been committing robberies dating back two years. My son and I sat at the kitchen table with this detective. That was the first time I saw my son smoke a cigarette. He was tight.

I looked in his face and asked him, "Did you do these robberies?"

He said, "Yes, Mommy."

"Well, then you must take ownership," I told him. We wrote a full confession and the judge sentenced him to 15 months in a group home. I started thinking, "Really, what can I do to parent this kid?" I thought back on the parenting and anger management classes I took when my kids were in care. I decided to create a parenting style for my son that I called, "Firm as a father, soft like a mother."

Keeping My Distance

When he got locked up, I let him do his time. I didn't run up to every visit or send packages and money. I didn't write letters or accept phone calls all the time. I was not in court for every court date. I didn't scream and beg and cry. I let him do hard time for 15 months, firm like a father.

I felt that running to his aid would enable him—it would give him extra attention for doing negative things—and I believed that would only encourage him to commit crimes again. If he got locked up, I'd come running.

When my son came home, he hugged me and kissed me. He said he had learned his lesson. I was glad I didn't cater to his nonsense and reckless choices. But once he was home, I began listening to him more, soft like a mother. I encouraged my son and held him to the standards he set for himself.

Soon my son dropped his gang activities, went back to school and got his GED. At 20, he is now a responsible father and is exploring starting his own business.

Trying Straight Talk

I faced similar challenges when my daughter was around 14 years old. My daughter was suddenly a whole new child. She began hanging with sexually experienced girls and started asking a lot of questions about boys.

I did my best to detour her from sex, but my best was not good enough. Soon I found out that my daughter was having sex with a 17-year-old boy. I was shocked, but I knew that if I overreacted, she would not open up to me, so I tried to play it cool.

We sat down in the living room and I asked her, "Why are you dealing with older boys and having sex right now? It seems like you're too young." I explained that I was not trying to take away the wonderful experience of sex, but that it is a sacred act for two people who love each other, and that I worried that the sex she was having could come with painful experiences, like unwanted pregnancy and STDs.

We didn't flip out on each other, but straight talk did not help my daughter.

Learning to Listen

She started cutting school and running away from home. It was so serious that I went to the child welfare system for help before they came to me, charging me for educational neglect because she was truant. The caseworker told me to put her in therapy and I reconnected her to our former foster care agency for therapy. But she went to three sessions and refused to go back.

Once again, I had to dig into my bag of parenting skills and find a way to reach her. I realized that my daughter didn't need tough love, she needed nurturing, compassion, connection.

I started having girl talk with my daughter. I didn't do much talking; I just listened openly. We even invited her runaway partners over to our house to have real heart-to-hearts. The other parents thanked me and tried the same thing.

My daughter is doing much better now. She stayed with my grandmother for two years and recently moved home again. She went back to school and her GPA went from a 40 to an 87. She applied to a college program in her high school and was accepted. She also got a job and is now working at our local supermarket. My daughter is doing well for herself.

No Child Is Alike

As teenagers, my children needed two different parenting styles. My son needed me to let him experience the consequences of his own mistakes. My daughter needed me to come closer. Both needed me to listen. My youngest child is 10 years old. I can't wait to see what style will help him thrive as he grows older. I've realized that no child is alike and no parenting model is right for all children.

I try to use patience, open-mindedness, understanding, empathy, nurturing, respect, kindness, honesty, courage, security and discipline. To be honest, these skills came from the many classes I completed while my children were in foster care. I'm thankful that I learned these skills. It needed more tools to deal with my children.

All Children Need Kindness

I believe parents should surrender the punitive parenting styles that they suffered as children. Adults who are good providers associate brutal beatings with their success. They tell their children, "It worked for me, it will work for you."

But we have learned that it doesn't really work. Children need to feel safe. They need your support to get ready to be responsible.

I understand that parents need to feel respected in their homes, and that learning new parenting skills takes diligence and practice. But I like the new model and use it. My children are doing better than they were. They're not perfect, but show me a child who is.

Rise

www.risemagazine.org

LEADER'S GUIDE:

'What Can I Do?' by Latonya Baskerville

My children needed me to try new ways to parent.

DISCUSSION FOCUS:

Positive discipline.

ACTIVITY GOAL:

Participants will identify new methods of responding to their children's behavior.

STORY SUMMARY

When Latonya's children came home from foster care, they were angry and running wild. Latonya did not know how to manage their behavior. She didn't want to hit her children but didn't know what to do besides yell.

Latonya thought back on parenting classes she had taken and thought about her children's needs. With her son, she set firm boundaries. With her daughter, she tried to be more nurturing. She also began to listen more to her children. Slowly, their relationships grew closer and her children's behavior improved.

DISCUSSION GUIDE

GROUP INTRODUCTION: 10 minutes

Today we're going to talk about our parenting styles and the tools we use to manage children's behavior. Children may act out to test you or to get your attention or love. When parents decide they don't want to discipline their children by hitting or yelling, they sometimes feel that they have no other tools. Communicating your expectations clearly and setting firm limits can help. So can nurturing and listening.

- How do you feel about this topic?
- Do you have experiences related to this topic that you'd like to share before we get started?

READ AND DISCUSS STORY: 15 + 30 minutes

Read the story out loud as a group. Help participants recognize the writer's emotions and coping mechanisms and their own. Go back over important moments in the story and ask the participants about how they've handled similar experiences:

STORY MOMENT	DISCUSSION QUESTION
Latonya doesn't want to hit her children or yell at them anymore.	What would you like to change about your parenting style?
Latonya feared that her son and daughter were putting themselves in danger.	What fears do you have about your children?
Latyonya decided not to give her son extra attention for negative behaviors.	How do you respond to your children's negative behaviors? How do you encourage positive behavior?
While her son responded to distance, Latonya felt her daughter needed more nurturing and closeness.	How could you listen to and nurture your children?
Latonya learns that listening to her children helps them feel secure.	What do you think is the connection between feeling secure and behaving well?

JOURNAL TIME: 15-30 minutes

By writing in their journals, participants can more deeply reflect on their own experiences. Hand out the "Journal Reflections" worksheet and give participants time to write. They can share their responses with the group or in pairs, or after the workshop with a peer, family member, therapist or other important person in their lives.

NAME: **DATE:**

JOURNAL REFLECTIONS: 'What Can I Do?' by Latonya Baskerville

When Latonya's children came home from foster care they felt angry and were running wild. Latonya felt she did not know how to parent them, but she did not give in to feeling guilty or respond to their behavior with harsh discipline. Latonya used limit setting, straight talk, nurturing and listening. Slowly their connection improved and so did her children's behavior. Write in your journal (or below) about strategies you can use to respond to your children's needs.

1. What concerns do you have about your children's behavior?

2. How do you typically respond to negative behavior?

3. How do you typically respond to positive behavior?

4. What concerns do you have about your parenting style? What do you do well?

____

____

____

____

ACTION STEPS

Latonya says that trying new skills takes diligence and patience. List 2-3 new skills you could try or use more often.

1. ____

____

____

2. ____

____

____

3. ____

____

____

A SUPPORTIVE CONNECTION

I plan to get support and encouragement by talking about my reflections and action steps with:

____

'Your History Is Not Destiny'

Most parents who were abused do not harm their kids.

Although people often talk about "breaking the cycle of abuse," studies show that most parents who were physically abused as children do not grow up to physically abuse their children, says Katherine Pears, a research scientist at the Oregon Social Learning Center. Here she explains the research on abuse and parenting:

That's a notion in people's heads that if you haven't had a good model of parenting, you're unlikely to become a good parent yourself.

But studies that have been going on for 20 years have looked at parents who were physically abused and how they care for their children, and most find that only 20-30 percent of people who were physically abused as children go on to be abusive. That means that at least 70 percent don't go on to be abusive.

A history of abuse is not destiny. It doesn't mean that you will grow up to have difficulties as a parent. There's a lot of room for hope.

Make a Rule a Rule

In my research, I found that one key to whether parents were physically abusive or not had to do with whether the parent was consistent in enforcing rules. I studied boys who had parents that had been abused, and found the parents who were inconsistent were more likely to be abusive.

Many parents find it difficult to remain consistent, but it's essential to be consistent as a parent. If something is a rule on Monday, but not on Tuesday, kids learn from that that they don't really have to mind what the parent says. Then, if the kid is not listening to the parent –well, that's annoying! The parent gets irritated.

If the parent backs off, that encourages the kid to be more negative next time, and that starts a negative cycle. The parent and child begin one-upping the other, hoping the other will back off, but sometimes the parent gets very angry and responds with aggression or abuse.

Consistent parenting keeps these negative cycles from developing. If a rule is a rule, and the child has to mind what the parent says all of the time, you nip that cycle in the bud.
Take Steps to Avoid Triggers
The hopeful message is that parents can

(Continued on next page)

(Continued from previous page)
learn techniques to stop the cycle. We teach the parent to be consistent and to use tools for reducing tension.

We teach parents to recognize triggers to negative interactions. If you tend to get in fights right after school, maybe you need a routine that will help you feel more positive. Can you have a snack together? Do you need a few minutes to cool off, or does your child? If you feel more positive, it's easier to be consistent about setting limits.

We also teach parents to take small steps. Say you want your child to put his backpack and lunchbox away when he comes home from school. We suggest taking small steps—first working with him on hanging up his backpack. Then, when he's doing well with his backpack, showing him how to put his lunchbox away.

Praise Your Child

We also know that one key to successful parenting is positive reinforcement. If you can catch your child doing something good, and praise your child for what he does well, then everyone feels better.

We ask parents, "What is your child doing well?" Even if it's just putting a plate on the counter without banging it, then you can say, "I noticed how you put your plate on the counter without banging!" If kids feel recognized for the things they do well, they are more willing to accept limits.

Programs that teach parents to set consistent limits, reduce triggers, and be positive with their children do help parents stop abusive patterns. Nobody is a lost cause. All parents can learn to be effective parents.

'I'm Sorry, My Son'

When my husband and I split up, my baby needed more than I could give.

By Yadira Fragoso

Translated from Spanish.

When my second son, Steven, was six months old, my husband and I separated. My life totally changed. I had to take care of Steven and his older brother, Stuart, who was only 2, and continue working in the restaurant where my husband, Pedro, also worked. That was the beginning of the worst period of my life.

Pedro and I had I started having some problems before I got pregnant with Steven. Pedro didn't want to have a second child, and I did.

Pedro had also started to go out fishing and playing soccer often. When the weekends would arrive, I'd say, "Let's go to the park with Stuart," and he'd say, "You bring him, because I'm tired." I would start to cry and I wouldn't bring him to the park because I was used to going everywhere with Pedro.

Separation and Depression

Even though our second child, Steven, was a baby we planned to have, things didn't go as well for our family after he was born. Pedro didn't always have work. When Steven was four months old, Pedro and I decided that we would both go to work in a restaurant to make more money.

I worked the night shift so that I could watch them in the morning and Pedro could take them at night. I felt like our married life was starting to come together economically, but emotionally, things weren't better between us, but worse. Finally, we split up.

After Pedro moved out, I fell into a depression, crying all the time and enduring terrible migraines.

To handle my feelings, I dedicated myself to my job and didn't pay a lot of attention to my sons. The worst part was seeing the difference in the lives of my two babies. Steven had to witness my arguments and my desperation, while as Stuart had grown older, he'd been able to share his life with his mother and father.

Close to Our Son

When Stuart was little, I had enjoyed motherhood a lot, and Pedro and I spent a lot of time with our son. We tried to give him the best childhood we could.

I wanted Stuart to become a very smart kid. I'd heard that if you talk to babies, telling them what you want them to become, it'll come true. So when he was just a little baby, I whispered in his ear while he was sleeping, saying, "Stuart, you have to be a very intelligent baby, and you should enjoy going to school a lot, so that when you are big you can have an important job where you want. Always be a good boy."

After a long search, I found a daycare for Stuart and I went back to work when he was 8 months old. Obviously it wasn't everything I might want in a daycare, but it was a place where I knew that they were going to take good care of him. It gave me a good feeling to see how Stuart continued growing. Right away, he started the typical game of saying, "Give me five," and with great enthusiasm he'd slap my hand!

Teaching Our Son at Home

Pedro and I were always finding ways teach him new things. When I took Stuart out shopping with me, I taught him the names of the fruits and vegetables, and said to him, "This is a car, a bus, a truck," and so on. Pedro and I also brought Stuart to the library to read, and borrowed books to read in the house.

When Stuart was almost a year old, I found out from a friend of mine about special classes for toddlers. I asked my social worker, but she said they were only for children with trouble speaking or with other problems. Even so, I asked for Stuart to get evaluated, and it turned out he could attend the special school. The school suggested that a teacher come to my home three times a week for an hour so that Stuart wouldn't forget what he learned.

When Stuart started his classes, I felt very good and content with myself as a mother. Over the two years he took them (until he turned 3 years old), I felt so proud of him. He learned the colors, numbers, and the ABCs, and improved so much in his speaking. I also asked Pedro if we could buy him English without Barriers for children so that Stuart could continue practicing English. Once the classes ended, I put on those videos, and through them, he learned new things.

'We'll Always Love You'

When I got pregnant with Steven, Pedro and I prepared Stuart by taking a book out of the library called, "The Baby's Arrival." I remember it well. It was the story of a pregnant mom who was ready to go to the hospital, and when the baby was born, returned home with the baby in her arms.

I said to Stuart, "Look, here under my tummy I have a baby that is going to be your brother, and when he's born, you shouldn't get angry, because your father and I will always love you." Stuart said to me, "Ok, Mami," and he hugged me and kissed my belly.

When I was almost ready to give birth to Steven, I asked Pedro if we could decorate the room so that it would look nice and give a good welcome to my Steven. Not much later, he was born.

'Where is Papi?'

When Pedro and I split up, my sons and I suffered a lot. It was up to me to help Stuart in the process of understanding our separation from his father. Stuart would ask me, "Where is my

Papi? I miss him." My tears flowed and I didn't know how to answer him. I'd invent excuses, like that he'd had to go work far away and that he was going to come back to see him and his brother.

But Steven suffered the most. During this time, I treated Steven as a child, not a baby. By that I mean that I would yell at him if he wanted something. If he cried, I would get annoyed and tell him to stop it. Sometimes when Steven wanted to play, I'd say, "Not now, I don't have time for that," or I'd ask Stuart to play with his little brother.

I remember one day that my Steven, when he was just 6 months, was crying and I got angry. I screamed, "All right, shut up now! What do you want?" and I left the room. I went to the kitchen and sat thinking, "What am I doing? He's a baby! He's not at fault for what happened." I felt so bad about the way I reacted.

Then I returned to the room crying, and I held him and said, "I'm sorry, my son, it's not your fault. I'm sorry." I hugged him and kissed him so many times until I felt better.

Of course, that's not how I treated him all the time. I also was loving. But it hurts me to realize how different I was with him than I was with Stuart.

My Babies Needed Me

I knew that that my sons' lives couldn't be OK if I wasn't OK. My babies needed me. They were the main reason I had to keep me from allowing myself to be completely defeated.

Fortunately, I had a number of people helping me so that I didn't fall apart completely. Thank God I could count on the support of my co-madre, Tere, and my sister, who both loved me so much.

I also continued with therapy and it helped me understand that my world didn't end with the separation and that I could become stronger day by day.

One day I arrived at my appointment undone, crying because I felt so bad. Unburdening myself to my therapist helped. She listened to me and said, "Yadira, you're a great woman, and I understand that you're sad—it's a difficult situation to confront—but everything will be OK. You can do it." Oh! Those words really made me feel good.

She suggested that I try to occupy my time taking the babies to the park and reading them a book every night, and I did that, trying to remain calm even when they misbehaved.

For a while I went out with a friend who was lovely with my babies and me. On Halloween, he accompanied me to buy costumes for Stuart and Steven, and we took them out to trick or treat. Although I felt happy while I was with him, when I returned home I felt flattened again.

Finally, I decided to take Stuart and Steven with me to Mexico for a year so we could live with my family. Being home with my mother, and dedicating more of my time to my sons, helped me a lot.

Still Feeling Guilty

After a year in Mexico, my sons and I moved back to New York in the fall.

Even though I'd say 75 percent of the depression I felt when Pedro and I separated has lifted, I still don't have as much time with my sons as I'd like because of the hours of my job. I wish I didn't have to work and I could stay at home teaching them and showing my love to my children.

Now Steven is 3 years old and I feel like I have given him more of my time. I always hold him close and kiss him, telling him, "You're my baby." (Although maybe that's not right, because now if Pedro asks him, "Are you my baby?" he says, "No." If Pedro says, "Are you Mama's baby?" he says, "Yes.")

My Steven seems a little bit restless and unsure of himself at times. If I want him to sit with me and draw or watch some children's videos together like I did with Stuart, he'll only be entertained for five minutes and then he'll get up and do something else.

I sit with him to do his homework, which is a little difficult, but we do it. I feel very proud of him because now that he goes to daycare, he's started to speak a few sentences in English.

Pedro tells me that Steven is a child that cries a lot and doesn't obey because whenever I yell at him, afterwards I soothe him. That might be true. What makes me do it is my sense of guilt that I didn't treat him like a baby when he needed me to.

I think that it's going to take a long time for this feeling of guilt to leave my heart. I still leave with the fear that Steven will reproach me for the difference in the way I treated him. I think I won't rest until I can hear my son, when he's older, tell me, "Don't feel bad about what happened, Mami. I understand."

Proud of Myself

Stuart is already 5 years old and graduating this spring from kindergarten. I feel proud of my sons, who are both so sweet and handsome. At night, we sing a lot of songs together. They tell me I'm the best mother in the world, and I feel proud of myself.

It's been three years since I was turned upside down, and I see that I'm on my feet, continuing my fight to move forward, and always in the company of my sons.

Rise

www.risemagazine.org

LEADER'S GUIDE:

'I'm Sorry, My Son' by Yadira Fragoso

When my husband and I split up, my son needed more than I could give.

DISCUSSION FOCUS:

Reestablishing a connection.

ACTIVITY GOAL:

Participants will recognize the impact of stress and depression on their children and the steps to becoming dependable again.

STORY SUMMARY

Yadira describes the challenges she faces parenting her children after she and their father split up. When her oldest son is younger, Yadira takes many steps to nurture and educate him but she has trouble responding to her younger son's needs after the separation because of depression and stress.

As she comes out of her depression, she tries to make it up to her younger son but at times still suffers from guilt.

DISCUSSION GUIDE

GROUP INTRODUCTION: 10 minutes

Today we'll talk about how kids are affected when parents feel unable to give them the attention they need. Parents may be incapable of responding to their children's needs for many reasons: depression, stress, addiction, domestic violence, or separations. Once a stressful period has passed, we may feel guilty and sad that we weren't able to do our best. We may see signs that our children were negatively affected by our physical or emotional absence—or worry that we do. Re-establishing normal routines and boundaries, and not letting guilt interfere with your parenting, helps get children back on track.

- How do you feel about this topic?
- Do you have experiences related to this topic that you'd like to share before we get started?

READ AND DISCUSS STORY: 15 + 30 minutes

Read the story out loud as a group. Help participants recognize the writer's emotions and coping mechanisms and their own. Go back over important moments in the story and ask the participants about how they've handled similar experiences:

STORY MOMENT	DISCUSSION QUESTION
Yadira enjoys motherhood when her older son is little and she is energetic about taking care of him.	What are your strengths as a parent?
When she becomes depressed, Yadira is less responsive to her children and expects too much.	When have you noticed that your expectations of your child were more than your child could handle?
When Yadira acts in a way she later feels badly about, she takes her son into her arms and kisses him all over.	How do you—or can you—make up with your child immediately after you act in a way that you regret?
Yadira's guilt and shame about not being emotionally available to her son when he was a baby sometimes lead her to baby her son now.	How do guilt or shame affect your parenting?
Yadira wishes she could make up for the past and is weighed down by her past behavior.	What is a positive way to apologize to your children for problems in the past and move forward?

JOURNAL TIME: 15-30 minutes

By writing in their journals, participants can more deeply reflect on their experiences and the steps they can take to strengthen themselves and their families. Hand out the "Journal Reflections" worksheet and give participants 15-30 minutes to write. They can share their responses with the group or in pairs, or after the workshop with a counselor, therapist, or peer.

NAME: **DATE:**

JOURNAL REFLECTIONS: 'I'm Sorry, My Son' by Yadira Fragoso

Yadira sees that her younger son, Steven, is more withdrawn than her older son, and she blames herself for the differences in their natures. She fears that Steven will blame her if he has problems when he is older. She feels unsure about how to be a good mother to him without babying him out of guilt.

Take some time to reflect on how you can help your children feel safe again after a difficult time and how you can forgive yourself. Use the questions below to guide your reflections.

1. What was a difficult time that you went through? How did it affect your parenting?

2. What concerns do you have about how that difficult time might have affected your children?

3. How did that difficult time affect your confidence as a parent?

4. What would help you regain your confidence and your children's confidence in you?

ACTION STEPS

Children feel best when family life returns to normal. It doesn't help to baby or pamper children out of guilt. At the same time, it can be difficult to forgive yourself. Write down 2-3 steps you can take to reestablish normalcy with your children and forgive yourself.

1.

2.

3.

A SUPPORTIVE CONNECTION

I plan to get support and encouragement by talking about my reflections and action steps with:

Help for the Whole Family

My son's learning disability affects us all.

By Debbie Echevarria

Translated from Spanish

My son Eric, who is 11, has a learning disability that makes it hard for him to stay focused and attentive. His disability affects not only his schoolwork but also our whole family.

Our family's long journey to figure out the problem Eric was having began when he was around 8 years old. He had been in a special classes for bright kids in 2nd and 3rd grade, but then he began to struggle.

We were having a hard time at home getting Eric to complete homework and chores. He was a playful child and always wanted to be the center of attention, sometimes achieving it in a negative way. He wouldn't finish his homework before starting to play, would occasionally be defiant and wouldn't go to bed on time.

Everyone Was Angry

I tried to make sure Eric completed his homework, but I felt my husband and my younger son, Brian, weren't helping me keep Eric on track. Brian would call Eric to play when I'd just said Eric needed to finish his homework first. My husband sometimes took the kids out to play before they completed their homework, as though it was every child's right to play any time.

My efforts to improve Eric's behavior put a huge strain on my family and on me. I got angry at my children when they didn't follow the rules. My husband also felt I wasn't attentive to him. I simply didn't have the time or energy. I'd tell them all, "If Eric just did his homework first, I would be happy and he would do well!"

Soon we were all angry at each other. My husband and Brian felt that they were being punished because of Eric, and Eric was always angry at me. He'd even say, "I hate you!" I was sad and yet determined to get Eric the help he needed at home and school.

Taking Steps

Eric's troubles seemed serious to me. As I struggled to understand my son, I read many books about children with Attention Deficit Disorder (ADD), Bipolar Disorder and communication problems. I felt it was important to learn about any of the problems that Eric might be going through and to think through my own conclusions before getting a professional involved in our family. But the books did not help me come to any conclusions.

So I visited the Center for Family Life in Sunset Park, which I knew about because it's in my neighborhood, and started to go to counseling with the children. (My husband couldn't come because of his work schedule.)

Rules and Chores

When we met the counselor, Nicole, I explained that we needed help as a family. I made it clear that we were not seeking help only for Eric, but that we needed to explore our family's patterns together.

Nicole was very supportive and my children were happy to speak with her. Nicole helped us address our difficulties in a few different ways. First she helped me implement a different way of getting my children to do chores. We made charts for the children to follow that listed their chores and responsibilities. That way it was clear what I expected from them.

Then we talked about some of the reasons that Eric, in particular, was having a hard time. Nicole felt that Eric was under too much pressure from his schoolwork. She also noticed that Eric felt bad about himself because he didn't fit in at school and he was having trouble making friends. Eric had alienated other children by being too friendly—he didn't know when to stop playing. So we tried different strategies to get Eric to feel good about his accomplishments.

Too Much Pressure

Nicole suggested that we consider removing Eric from the gifted program and putting him in a less stressful environment. It was a tough decision, because he was already feeling bad about himself. But that was something he needed.

We also tried new ways to help him keep focused. I started to notice that Eric was having trouble in class and with friends because he often blurted out his first thoughts. Nicole worked with Eric to teach him to slow down and think before answering questions, and to learn not to be overconfident.

I also started to read books with him when I realized he was reading too quickly to absorb important information. I read short stories to Eric and found that taking turns reading was helpful in slowing him down. After we read out loud together, it was easier to discuss the story, and his understanding of his schoolwork improved.

A Little Change

My family and I were very happy to see some progress. We noticed Eric was thinking more about what he said, so he had more to feel good about, and that made everyone a little less stressed.

But after six months we had to stop seeing Nicole because she left the Center. We didn't move on to a new counselor. Even though Eric was still struggling, he and Brian were happier and enjoying our time together with family.

But in July 2005, I visited the Center again because, once more, the kids were misbehaving and my husband and I were upset.

Trying Again

Our new social worker was named Andrea. She arranged for Eric to get a psychological evaluation to determine if he had ADD or some other disorder. The psychologist suggested that he be evaluated for verbal communication, so he saw a speech therapist and had his hearing and vision checked.

I also had him evaluated for what's called a "central auditory processing disorder," a problem that makes it difficult to block out background noise. My niece's son had the disorder, and as it turned out, Eric also was diagnosed with it.

We found out that this disability makes it hard to focus on what one person is saying if there is any background noise. Obviously, if you don't block out background noise very well, it's hard to concentrate on the teacher's voice in school. This diagnosis has gotten Eric the help he needed, and that's helped our family life a lot.

A Helpful Diagnosis

The first step in treatment was for Eric to use an "FM unit" at school. That means the teacher wears a microphone on her shirt that transmits her voice straight to an earpiece that Eric wears. This enables him to hear only his teacher, drowning out the sound of other children and distractions. It has helped him thrive.

Eric also has seen two speech therapists. Part of the problem is that Eric has trouble keeping information in the proper sequence in his mind. The speech therapists help Eric to learn and practice sequencing and that's enabled him to be more organized.

I am relieved that we finally got a correct diagnosis and happy to see Eric finally get the help he needs. Eric is relieved as well, but he has also felt confused and a little sad about having a disability.

A Kinder Approach

The biggest change is in how Eric is treated in school. Before Eric was diagnosed, he had a terrible year. His teachers insisted that he simply had a discipline problem. He was in trouble all the time and ended up repeating 5th grade.

Now the teachers understand that Eric's behavior was part of a disability, and they see that his behavior is improving now that he uses the FM unit.

We've had to teach Eric to ask the teachers for what he needs. When he first started using the FM unit, sometimes Eric would tell me, "Mom, the teacher didn't use the FM unit today. She had it off all the time."

I tried to help him understand that he needed to advocate for himself. "Eric, you must let her know that she doesn't have it on, or else she won't know," I'd say. While Eric still believes his teacher picks on him, he has been able to speak up and ask for what he needs.

Working Hard

Eric is feeling better about himself because he's able to do better in school and at home. I feel proud of Eric because he is working hard. He's also becoming a more understanding, loving and tender child.

The help that Eric and our whole family have gotten has not solved everything. At home, my younger son still feels left out because he doesn't get as much attention as Eric, and sometimes he can be pretty rebellious.

My husband and I try to keep both kids happy and treat them equally, even though Eric has turned out to have more needs than Brian. We need a great deal of patience.

I'm not feeling as stressed, frustrated and angry now that I better understand Eric's behavior. I'm a happier mother. With Eric getting the help he needs at school, I am able to dedicate more time to my whole family.

But I think our family still needs support. My husband and I will soon begin counseling with Andrea so we can continue to work with each other and the kids in a positive way and so we can feel confident that Eric and Brian will grow up to become independent, responsible adults.

Rise

www.risemagazine.org

LEADER'S GUIDE:

Help for the Whole Family by Debbie Echevarria

My son's learning disability affects us all.

DISCUSSION FOCUS:

Getting professional help.

ACTIVITY GOAL:

Participants will define behaviors they are concerned about and reflect on their own attitudes toward counseling.

STORY SUMMARY

When Debbie's son begins to struggle in school and at home, everyone in her family ends up angry at each other. Debbie searches for supports that will help her son, who turns out to have a disability that's making it hard for him to pay attention in school.

Debbie finds the treatment her son needs and brings her children to family therapy in order to put her family back on track.

DISCUSSION GUIDE

GROUP INTRODUCTION: 10 minutes

Today we'll talk about getting professional help when your children need more help than you can give them. When children are having serious behavioral problems in school or at home, it may be that they are suffering from a learning disability, mental illness, or medical problem that is interfering with their ability to learn or behave appropriately. Children's disabilities affect a whole family. Siblings can feel jealous of the attention and parents may feel exhausted. In addition to treatment that a child needs to help with the disability, parents or families may need family therapy or counseling.

- How do you feel about this topic?
- Do you have experiences related to this topic that you'd like to share before we get started?

READ AND DISCUSS STORY: 15 + 30 minutes

Read the story out loud as a group. Help participants recognize the writer's emotions and coping mechanisms and their own. Go back over important moments in the story and ask the participants about how they've handled similar experiences:

STORY MOMENT	DISCUSSION QUESTION
Everyone was affected by stress because Eric was having trouble doing his homework and chores.	How have you seen in your own families that a problem facing one person can affect everyone?
At first, Debbie felt that everyone was working against her as she tried to help Eric succeed in school.	When have you felt alone with a family problem?
Debbie found support by going to family therapy.	How do you think a counselor or therapist could help your family during a crisis?
Debbie was persistent in looking for help for Eric and her family.	How have you advocated—or could you advocate—for yourself and your family?
Debbie says, "I am not feeling as stressed, frustrated and angry now that I better understand Eric's behavior."	How did you get help when you couldn't understand your child's behavior?

JOURNAL TIME: 15-30 minutes

By writing in their journals, participants can more deeply reflect on their experiences and the steps they can take to strengthen themselves and their families. Hand out the "Journal Reflections" worksheet and give participants 15-30 minutes to write. They can share their responses with the group or in pairs, or after the workshop with a counselor, therapist, or peer.

NAME: **DATE:**

JOURNAL REFLECTIONS: Help for the Whole Family by Debbie Echevarria

Debbie feels happier as a mother after she finds the right treatment for her son, who has a disability. Take time to reflect on the concerns you have about your children and whether a family therapist could help you or your child with difficult behaviors. Use the questions below to guide your reflections.

1. What concerns do you have about your children's behavior or schoolwork?

2. How do you think your family life is affected by these issues?

3. How do you feel about seeking professional help for your child?

4. How might family counseling help you as well as your children?

____

____

____

____

ACTION STEPS

Many parents have fears about seeing a counselor. Your peers or someone you trust at a religious or community organization or at your child's school can help you find family supports you can trust. Write down 2-3 steps you can take if your family could use additional help.

1. ____

____

____

2. ____

____

____

3. ____

____

____

A SUPPORTIVE CONNECTION

I plan to get support and encouragement by talking about my reflections and action steps with:

____

Far From Home

I needed help that my family couldn't give me.

By Evelyn Salazar

Translated from Spanish.

Two years after my son was born, I decided I couldn't continue my relationship with his father and we separated. I was sad and confused, but Rene and I were arguing all the time and I knew ending it would be the best for my son and me. I said to myself, "Don't confuse a fear of loneliness with love."

It was one of the most difficult moments in my life, especially because I was far from home with few friends to lean on. I'd come to New York from Mexico with only my cousin when I was barely 16 years old. My mother asked me to come here so I could help our family economically.

When I first arrived, I felt sad but excited to be in another country earning money for my family. I found a job and made a group of friends that I had fun going out with. Then I met Rene and we had our son, Dylan. Soon I became distant from my friends without realizing it, and my son and his father became my world.

More Alone Than Ever

After Rene and I split up, it was difficult to wake up knowing that I was alone in New York without my mother, siblings or friends, without my father who died when I was young, and without Rene by my side. I came here full of dreams, feeling strong. Only six years later, I found myself without the friends I'd made or the family I'd created, sad and disillusioned. I felt unsure of how I could move forward without anyone to confide in or to support me, and with my beautiful baby depending on me to provide for him.

I thought about returning to Mexico. But I told myself, "Evelyn, what are you going to do there? It will only be harder to help your family economically if you go back home."

I also told myself that I would not flee my problems. I would face the challenges in front of me. I wanted to teach Dylan that no matter what happened his mother was going to fight to get ahead.

'If My Mama Was Here...'

Dylan and I moved to the only apartment I could afford—we share it with three strangers. I brought Dylan to a babysitter every morning and I worked at a coffee shop from 7 a.m. to 3 p.m. so I could spend afternoons with him.

At first, simple things felt so hard without a partner. If I had to go to the corner store because Dylan wanted his glass of milk before going to sleep, I'd have to take him with me, even in the winter when we had to wrap ourselves up in heavy clothing. I worried about Dylan while I bathed. Always I returned to the same thing: "If my Mami was here maybe she could stay with him and I would have time and freedom."

I could hardly find time for myself and I couldn't distract myself from my worries like I could when I was single. At times, I had invitations to go dancing, to eat out, or simply do something quiet. It was frustrating to turn down the things I craved.

Feeling Stuck

Sometimes I felt angry at Dylan, at myself, and at my family in Mexico. As a single mother and an illegal immigrant, I was struggling with the fear that I couldn't follow my dream of going to college and finding a better job.

Then I could only say, "Oh my God, forgive me, Dylan, please, my baby, I feel bad for thinking that, because now that I am not a free woman, things can't go as easily for me."

I'd feel a terrible sadness for thinking that my child was impeding my progress, because in truth, I felt fortunate to have a son, especially one as enchanting and marvelous as Dylan.

I felt as if I had one side of a coin and I wanted both and was going around and around all the time. I loved when I could stop a moment and look at my baby. At times I would say, "Dylan," and with his little boy voice he'd answer, "What, Mama?" I'd look at his eyes and wonder if there was sadness in his heart. My eyes would feel weak and before a tear could run from them, I'd say, "You know what, my love? You're the love of my life, my great treasure."

'You Can Do It'

To find a better job, I went to a center in my neighborhood where they help people find work. But because I don't have papers, they couldn't help me. They told me about other free services that I could get despite my immigration status, such as English classes, help filing taxes, or family counseling.

I thought a counselor could help me because I didn't have many friends and I wanted someone who could listen objectively to my story. I didn't speak with my family about my sadness and loneliness. Every time I spoke to them they were so focused on unburdening themselves of their own problems or looking to me to help them, and I preferred to keep my sad feelings to myself.

So I began going with Dylan to counseling at the Center for Family Life in Sunset Park. My counselor, Liza, took the time to listen to me and help me with my decisions and thoughts. She also helped me find a good daycare for Dylan and he thrived there.

Counseling gave me time to get to know myself better. I had so many things on my mind, and so much to do, that I hadn't taken time to relax and make myself think more calmly about my feelings and priorities. Liza encouraged me, saying, "You'll be OK, keep going. You can do it, you are doing it and you'll achieve your goals." For me these words were incredibly important and validating.

Connecting Little by Little

Little by little, I also started to make a social life. You meet so many people, but only with a few are you going to find a real closeness. I said to myself, "If the people who invite me out take off because I have a son, I'm better off even though it hurts. I don't need to be with someone who doesn't understand me or make me feel good."

I found that while some turned their backs, others opened their doors for me and my son. I don't have too many friends now, but the ones I have are good friends. They are people in whom I can confide and who also confide in me.

Over time, my relationship with Rene has changed, too. We appreciate each other now as friends. I am very proud of him as a father.

It took us a long time to get to this point. At times I felt like my efforts were useless, but I kept going and told myself, "Even if he doesn't want something good, I do, and I will keep trying." Now he takes Dylan twice a week, and he knows me and cares about me as a person. He tells me, "Evelyn, you're a good, smart, strong girl. If anyone deserves for good things to happen to her, it's you."

Many Steps Forward

Last winter, I took a big step toward reaching my dreams. I enrolled in college, and I've been taking three or four classes a semester since then.

I am very happy that I am studying because this is something I always dreamed of, but it's also a difficult task to study, work, and be a mother, friend, and daughter at the same time without allowing myself to fall at the first obstacle.

We have so many more expenses now that I'm paying for school and books. I am ineligible for financial aid because of my immigration status, so I have to pay the full bill. But I am able to afford school because our rent is low. The main drawback is that I can't send much money to my mother. I try to send her money for special occasions or in an emergency.

I go to school three times a week, usually bringing Dylan to the daycare there. It would be better if he didn't have to spend so much time in school and daycare, but I don't have many options, so I follow the phrase, "Quality is better than quantity." The days I am with him I am by his side the whole time.

Our Own World

Now when it's just Dylan and me, it's like we're in our own world. He likes to ask me strange and serious questions, like, "What if the moon was in a different space? And why is it always following us?" or, "What does the word 'criminal' mean? Because I heard it in the movie Spider-man." These questions throw me for a loop, but I search for words that, at his age, he can understand.

In nice weather we go to the park, ride bikes, skate, or go to the playground. At home, we play with toys, draw, watch TV, read, sing and sometimes exercise together—we do Pilates. Some days I have too much homework and can't give him my time all afternoon, so I tell him, "Ok, Dylan, we'll play but only for a short time because then Mami has to do something else." While I do my homework, he does his, or he draws, and afterward we eat together and go to sleep.

I try to bring my son happiness every day. When I'm reading him a story, I try to perform each of the characters with enthusiasm. Many times I'm very tired, and at first it wasn't easy for me to make time, but both he and I are adjusting.

Dylan and I are calmer now and our relationship is more stable. We chat more together and play more pleasantly, and at the same time, I don't feel I'm neglecting myself as I used to.

A Chance to Grow

I have so much more I want to achieve. I would like to move to a better apartment and find a better job. But I can't solve every problem right this minute. I try not to stress myself out thinking about what I want and can't have. I am trying to take things more calmly and to go forward little by little.

Some days I feel angry at the injustices I face. If I could become a legal citizen, I know I would be able to do so many things. I feel powerless knowing that I can't do anything to change my immigration status. It's out of my hands. I only hope with great faith that one day my immigration status won't stand in my way.

When I am thinking positively, I look back on this painful time and say, "Maybe I needed some solitude to focus on my son and myself." I don't feel as strongly that becoming a single parent is holding me back. These years have helped me grow as a woman and a mother.

Rise

www.risemagazine.org

LEADER'S GUIDE:

Far From Home by Evelyn Salazar
I needed help that my family couldn't give me.

DISCUSSION FOCUS:
Parent self-care.

ACTIVITY GOAL:
Participants will identify sources of support in their lives and places they could turn in a crisis.

STORY SUMMARY

When Evelyn separates from her son's father, she is overwhelmed by the challenges of raising her son alone. Her family in Mexico relies on her to support them, while Evelyn has no one to support her as a single parent in America. She loves her son, but sometimes she feels he is holding her back.

Over time, though, Evelyn finds sources of support and begins to balance being a good mother to her son and moving forward with her own life.

DISCUSSION GUIDE

GROUP INTRODUCTION: 10 minutes
Today we're going to talk about how important it is for parents to take care of themselves. In order to be open and caring toward your children, you must feel nurtured and supported yourself. Parents need time to themselves as well as people they can turn to for support and insight into their children's behavior. It can be difficult to build supportive relationships, particularly if you've had painful experiences trusting family members, friends, or partners. Building a strong support network is a long process, and you may even need help from a counselor as you try to let people into your life in a safe way.

- How do you feel about this topic?
- Do you have experiences related to this topic that you'd like to share before we get started?

READ AND DISCUSS STORY: 15 + 30 minutes

Read the story out loud as a group. Help participants recognize the writer's emotions and coping mechanisms and their own. Go back over important moments in the story and ask the participants about how they've handled similar experiences:

STORY MOMENT	DISCUSSION QUESTION
After separating from an abusive partner, Evelyn knows she needs help getting her life back on track.	Who have you turned to when you wanted help moving forward in your life?
Evelyn cannot turn to her own family because they have their own concerns.	How does feeling isolated or unsupported affect your parenting?
Evelyn needs support with conflicting feelings: love for her son and resentment that caring for him keeps her from reaching her own goals.	What help would you like with setting and reaching goals?
Evelyn turns to therapy because she needs someone to listen to her without judgment.	How would you feel about turning to a counselor for support?
Therapy helps Evelyn feel more capable of making friendships and building a positive partnership with her son's father.	What might help you strengthen your support network?

JOURNAL TIME: 15-30 minutes

By writing in their journals, participants can more deeply reflect on their experiences and the steps they can take to strengthen themselves and their families. Hand out the "Journal Reflections" worksheet and give participants 15-30 minutes to write. They can share their responses with the group or in pairs, or after the workshop with a counselor, therapist, or peer.

NAME: **DATE:**

JOURNAL REFLECTIONS: Far From Home by Evelyn Salazar

Evelyn went to counseling to give herself time to focus on herself. Nurturing herself allowed her to enjoy time with her son instead of feeling overwhelmed by the pressures of caring for him alone.

Take some time to think about how you could take time to care for yourself and how you could seek the support you might need or want. Use the questions below to guide your reflections.

1. How does feeling isolated or stressed affect the way you care for your children?

2. What activities help you feel calm and taken care of?

3. How do you make time for yourself or how you could make more time to take care of your own needs?

4. Who are your strongest supporters and how do they support you?

ACTION STEPS

You may be able to get more support from the people close to you by asking them directly for the help you need. Write down 2-3 things you could ask of your friends and family during a difficult time.

1.

2.

3.

A SUPPORTIVE CONNECTION

I plan to get support and encouragement by talking about my reflections and action steps with:

Acknowledgments

Healing Ourselves, Healing Our Children was developed with generous support from Hedge Funds Care and the Child Welfare Fund. Hedge Funds Care supported Rise in developing resources for parent education classes and parent support groups. The Child Welfare Fund provided general support to work with parents to write their stories.

The Center for Family Life in Sunset Park collaborated with Rise to develop the stories and discussion guides in this book. Social worker Liza Blank designed and co-facilitated a conversation and writing group for mothers in Sunset Park. Liza also collaborated with Rise to develop the guide topics and activities and ran a parenting support group using stories in this book. Thank you, Liza, for your generosity, insight and hard work.

Stories by Evelyn, Margarita, Maribel and Margarita were originally written in Spanish. Thank you to Ernesto Fedukovitch and Lisandro Perez Rey for proofreading our Spanish stories. For stories in Spanish, go to http://www.risemagazine.org/pages/en-espanol.html.

We developed our method of working with parent writers through work with our longtime partners, the Child Welfare Organizing Project and Youth Communication. CWOP is a parent / professional partnership dedicated to public child welfare reform in New York City through increased, meaningful parent involvement in service and policy planning. Thanks to Teresa Bachiller, Mike Arsham and many parents at CWOP for supporting Rise. Youth Communication publishes *Represent*, a magazine by and for youth in foster care, and incubated Rise. Many thanks to YC staff Jeff Faerber, Laura Longhine, Loretta Chan, Tom Brown, Efrain Reyes and Keith Hefner for lending their expertise to Rise.

Finally, Rise is indebted to all of the parents who chose to write about their experiences. It's not easy to share the many private struggles we all face with our children or to spend weeks developing stories paragraph by paragraph. Thank you for your courage in writing stories that are thoughtful, useful and beautiful.

Rise

NEW PARENTING RESOURCES from RISE

REUNIFICATION

IT WON'T HAPPEN AGAIN

Stories about reunification by parents affected by the child welfare system

#CW-REUN, 82 pp. $12.00

When children act out after reunification, parents often feel overwhelmed. Help parents understand children's fear and anger and learn healthy responses that other parents have used to repair relationships with their children.

• 9 stories by parents who have reunified with their children

• Discussion guides for each story—use in staff training, parenting classes, or parent support groups

• Worksheets for each story to help parents reflect on their experiences and define "action steps" they can take to handle the stresses of reunification

---

PARENTING SKILLS

HEALING OURSELVES, HEALING OUR CHILDREN

Stories about parenting by parents affected by the child welfare system

#CW-HIST, 86 pp. $12.00

Parents who grew up with chaos, trauma, or family separation need guidance to build safe, nurturing homes. Parents will feel capable of setting routines, improving communication, and using positive discipline when they read these stories by their peers.

• 10 stories by child welfare-affected parents

• Discussion guides for each story—use in staff training, parenting classes, or support groups

• 2 interviews with child welfare experts

• Worksheets for each story to help parents reflect on their experiences and define "action steps" they can take to strengthen their families

PARENT-FOSTER PARENT RELATIONSHIPS

BUILDING A BRIDGE

Stories about building collaboration between parents and foster parents

#CW-BRD, 130 pp. $18.95

Positive relationships between parents and foster parents help children feel more secure in care and adjust more easily after reunification.

Building a Bridge includes:

- 10 stories by parents
- 5 stories by foster parents
- 5 stories by teens
- 2 interviews with child welfare experts
- 14 Leader's Guides give you step-by-step instructions for using the stories in groups.

FOUR EASY WAYS TO ORDER

1 Order Via the Web
24 HOURS A DAY
www.risemagazine.org/pages/resources.html

2 Fax Your Order
24 HOURS A DAY
212-279-8856

3 Mail Your Order
Rise/Youth Communication
224 W. 29th Street, 2nd floor
New York, NY 10001

4 Phone Your Order
212-279-0708
x115

Ship To: (No PO Boxes)

Name____________________

Title____________________

Organization____________________

Address____________________

City__________State____Zip______

Phone/e-mail____________________

☐ Check Enclosed ☐ Bill me (P.O. must be enclosed)

☐ Credit Card

Visa/Master Card American Express Discover (circle one)

Card #____________________ Exp date________

Cardholder name exactly as it appears on card (please print)

Cardholder Signature

Healing Ourselves	# of books	Total
1-24 @ $12.00 each	____	____
25-49 @ $11.00 each	____	____
50 or more $10.00 each	____	____

It Won't Happen Again	# of books	Total
1-24 @ $12.00 each	____	____
25-49 @ $11.00 each	____	____
50 or more $10.00 each	____	____

Building a Bridge	# of books	Total
1-24 @ $18.95 each	____	____
25-49 @ $16.95 each	____	____
50 or more $12.95 each	____	____

Shipping & Handling
$5 on orders up to $100
$10 on orders $101-$249
$15 on orders above $250

Shipping ______

Total ______

CPSIA information can be obtained at www.ICGtesting.com
Printed in the USA
BVOW09s2058100416

443732BV00001B/2/P

9 781933 939995